Educated at St Paul's School, John Adair has enjoyed a varied and colourful career. He served in the Arab Legion, worked as a deckhand on an Arctic trawler and had a spell as an orderly in a hospital operating theatre. After Cambridge he became Senior Lecturer in Military History and Leadership Training Adviser at the Royal Military Academy, Sandhurst, before becoming Director of Studies at St George's House in Windsor Castle and then Associate Director of The Industrial Society.

In 1979 John became the world's first university Professor of Leadership Studies at the University of Surrey. He holds the degrees of Master of Arts from Cambridge University, Master of Letters from Oxford University and Doctor of Philosophy from London University, and he also is a Fellow of the Royal Historical Society.

In 2006 the People's Republic of China conferred on John the title of Honorary Professor of Leadership Studies in recognition of his 'outstanding research and contribution in the field of Leadership'. In 2009 the United Nations appointed him to be Chair of Strategic Leadership Studies at its central college in Turin.

www.johnadair.co.uk
www.adairleadershipdevelopment.com

EFFECTIVE LEADERSHIP

HOW TO BE A SUCCESSFUL LEADER

JOHN ADAIR

PAN BOOKS

First published 1983 by Gower Publishing Co. Ltd
This edition published 2009 by Pan Books
an imprint of Pan Macmillan Ltd
Pan Macmillan, 20 New Wharf Road, London N1 9RR
Basingstoke and Oxford
Associated companies throughout the world
www.panmacmillan.com

ISBN 978-0-330-50419-5

1 3 5 7 9 8 6 4 2

A CIP catalogue record for this book is available
from the British Library.

Typeset by Setsytems Ltd, Saffron Walden, Essex
Printed and bound in the UK by
CPI Mackays, Chatham ME5 8TD

CONTENTS

FOREWORD

Welcome to this fully revised second edition of *Effective Leadership*. The book first appeared in 1983 and it has been continuously in print ever since.

Authors sometimes spoil their best book when it comes to revising and updating it. My approach has been a cautious one. Rather like a good picture restorer I have limited myself to removing old varnish and flaking paint, and touching up here or there with new examples and case studies, so that you may encounter the original in all its simplicity, colour and freshness.

I hope that the book will serve you better as a wise guide, a firm support and an encouraging friend as you progress upon the path of leadership.

John Adair
2009

INTRODUCTION

Ideas about leadership have changed considerably in recent times. People today are better educated and more articulate. They can no longer be commanded or bossed about in the same way as before. Throughout the world there is a growing need for 'good leaders and leaders for good'. That is the background for our journey together in these pages.

The aim of this book is simple. It is to help you to improve your own abilities as a leader.

I am assuming that you have a direct personal interest in leadership. You may be in a position which you suspect – or have been told – requires leadership. You may already be an experienced leader, or you may be on the threshold of a career in management in which you will be expected to become a leader. In each case, leadership matters to you.

How can you improve your leadership ability?

- **You need to stimulate your own *awareness* of leadership in all its aspects.** That means being aware of when it is required in a given situation and aware of when it is lacking. It also entails an awareness of the changing values of society (and industry, which reflects those values), which will deepen your awareness of the importance of good leadership if free men and women are to cooperate effectively.

- **You need to establish your *understanding* of the principles, requirements or functions of leadership.** The poor leadership of many managers can be attributed, in part, to ignorance. No one ever introduced them to the functions of leadership, so they miss out some vital factor. A good leader understands the whole spectrum of leadership behaviour, and knows when a given function is required.

- **You need to develop your *skills* in providing the necessary functions.** This book will give you guidance not only on when to do a particular action, and why it should be done, but also how it should be done. It is concerned with techniques in a wide sense, namely the *methods* you must practise in order to achieve your desired aim of becoming a better leader. But this book will not teach you much about techniques in the narrower sense – the formal or mechanical tricks which are often taught at the expense of the art of leadership as a whole. Concentrate on the basics – and leave the tricks of the trade to the charlatans.

By the time you have finished the book I hope to have aroused or deepened your interest in leadership, to have persuaded you that there is an inner core of structure to it, and to have prompted you to see ways in which you can develop your own ability to the full.

HOW TO USE THIS BOOK

In order to get the most from this book it is best to read it once to get a general understanding. Then go back and work through the checklist questions and exercises. If you can persuade a friend or colleague to monitor your answers, so much the better.

Do not assume that you have to start from the beginning and read through to the end. The book is organized to move from the general to the more particular; from the whole to the specific part. Some people prefer to learn by starting off with the particular (e.g. drills, skills or techniques) and moving to general. If you belong to this group it may be better for you to start with Part Two and work hard on that, then read Part One. The more general ideas in Part Three are designed to stimulate further thought. You may also prefer to complete the checklists at the end of most chapters *before* reading the chapter rather than afterwards. Decide your strategy for using the book now, according to your depth of interest and preferred method of learning.

HOW WE LEARN

Regardless of which approach you adopt or how carefully you read this book, you will learn nothing about leadership unless you make a conscious effort to relate the points to your real life experience. It is essential to bear in mind that people learn by the interaction of

PRINCIPLES		EXPERIENCE
or	and	or
THEORY		PRACTICE

It is when sparks jump between these two poles – the general and the actual – that learning occurs. So you need both. The various case studies and examples in this book are designed to be 'stepping stones':

PRINCIPLES → THIRD-PERSON → *YOUR*
　　　　　　　EXAMPLES 　　*EXPERIENCE*

Equally, the process must work in reverse. Your practical knowledge, gleaned from both observation of actual leaders and your own practical experience, must be brought to bear in a constructively critical way on the ideas presented in this book.

So read the book reflectively. Put it down occasionally and work on some incidents in your own career which are illuminated by the book, since personal reflections will illustrate leadership lessons better than any second-hand case study.

The value of having some principles, guidelines or checklists of leadership is that they will cut down the time you take to learn from experience. As Henry Ford said, 'By the time a man is ready to graduate from the University of Experience he is too old to work!' George Bernard Shaw added that the fees you have to pay in that hard school are exceptionally high! Nothing can prevent you from making your own mistakes, for book learning is not the same as practical wisdom. But trial and error is an expensive and over-long way of learning about leadership: it is cheaper and saves time if you learn from other people's mistakes. The beginner in leadership should look upon this book as a 'sketch map' of an undiscovered country. The real terrain will not always look like the rough map in one's hand. In time one will be able to draw a better map, but at least this serves as a guide.

Of course, nothing can rival what we learn by experience. This book may not teach the veteran leader anything new, but it may help him or her to place in better order what they know already, so that they can make better use of it. The Three Circles model (page 38) is especially valuable

here. It serves as the core of my own understanding of
leadership.

USING THE BOXES

This book is primarily a practical guide, but I hope that it
will also be enjoyable to read. To supplement the main
body of the text I have introduced in the boxes what
amounts to a small anthology on leadership. My main
objective in doing so is to stimulate further thought by giving some tangible examples of what proven and often
famous leaders have done or said. Some have appeared in
my earlier books but I have called them into service again
because they are classic illustrations. I have boxed them so
that if you prefer you can omit them altogether without
missing the main points; however, the effort on your part
to relate the examples in the boxes to the ideas in the text
should prove rewarding. This could be a further exercise to
set yourself at the end of your preliminary reading.

You will notice that I have chosen to quote mainly from
actual leaders rather than from academics; the reason being
that I find them far more useful. But the fact that some of
these pieces are by military men calls for comment. Am I
advocating a military style of leadership in all human enterprises? Of course not. Leadership is not military, male or
western by origin: it is a universal human phenomenon.

Yet the materials of leadership – the qualities, functions
and principles – are the same in any field of work. I am
assuming that you have sufficient creative intelligence to
search for lessons about leadership in areas other than your
own work sphere. For to become an educated leader as well
as a trained one you need a 'wide span of relevance'. There
will be a *principle* or general method in these examples from

history or another field which is relevant to you. You have to identify that principle with my help and *transfer* or translate it to the context of your own field. I hope that the examples I give will prompt you to start your own anthology of leadership, as a personal supplement to these pages.

PART ONE

UNDERSTANDING LEADERSHIP

Understanding, for most people, is the key that unlocks the door of action. You need to know about the findings of research in this field and to accept or formulate some general or integrated concept of leadership. This knowledge will then serve as a guide or sketch map as you explore further the question of leadership later in the book.

By the time you have finished reading the sections and working on the various checklists, exercises and case studies in Part One, you should:

- know the three main approaches to leadership and be able to see how they fit together into the general theory of leadership based upon the Three Circles model (see page 38)
- have become more aware of how the three areas of **task**, **team** and **individual** interact with each other, for good or ill
- see that leadership is done on various levels, such as – in the context of organizations – **team, operational** and **strategic leadership.**

1

WHAT YOU HAVE TO BE OR BECOME

'Reason and calm judgement,
the qualities especially belonging to a leader.'
Tacitus

It is a fact that some men possess an inbred superiority which gives them a dominating influence over their contemporaries, and marks them out unmistakably for leadership. This phenomenon is as certain as it is mysterious. It is apparent in every association of human beings, in every variety of circumstances and on every plane of culture. In a school among boys, in a college among the students, in a factory, shipyard or a mine among the workmen, as certainly as in the Church and in the Nation, there are those who, with an assured and unquestioned title, take the leading place, and shape the general conduct.

So declared Hensley Henson, Bishop of Durham, in a lecture on leadership delivered at the University of St Andrews in Scotland in 1934. Since time immemorial people have sought to understand this natural phenomenon of leadership. What is it that gives a person this influence over his or her fellows?

As this lecturer believed, most people thought that leadership was an 'inbred superiority' – in other words, you are either born with it or not. The born leader will emerge naturally as the leader because his qualities of mind, spirit and character give him that 'assured and unquestioned title'. (Notice, incidentally, the universal unconscious assumption of former times that leadership is always a male prerogative.) Since 1934 quite a lot of leaders, observers of leaders, and trainers of leaders have been prepared to list the qualities which they believe constitute born leadership. The difficulty is that the lists vary considerably, even allowing for the fact that the compilers are often using rough synonyms for the same trait. They also become rather long. In fact there is a bewildering number of trait names from which the student of leadership could make up his or her portfolio. There are some 17,000 words in the English language which can be used for describing personality or character.

A study by Professor Charles Bird of the University of Minnesota in 1940 looked at twenty experimental investigations into leadership and found that only 5 per cent of the traits described appeared in three or more of the lists.

A questionnaire survey of seventy-five top executives, carried out by the American business journal *Fortune*, listed fifteen executive qualities: judgement, initiative, integrity, foresight, energy, drive, human relations skill, decisiveness, dependability, emotional stability, fairness, ambition, dedication, objectivity and cooperation. Nearly a third of the seventy-five said that they thought all these qualities were indispensable. The replies showed that these personal qualities have no generally accepted meaning. For instance, the definitions of dependability included 147 different concepts. Some executives even gave as many as eight or nine.

Apart from this apparent confusion, there is a second drawback to the qualities or traits approach: it does not form a good basis for leadership development. 'Smith is not a born leader yet,' wrote one manager about his subordinate. What can the manager do about it? What can Smith do? The assumption that leaders are born and not made favours an emphasis upon *selection* rather than *training* for leadership. It tends to favour early identification of those with the silver spoon of innate leadership in their mouths and it breeds the attitude 'you cannot teach leadership'. However, this assumption has now been challenged and proven to be false.

Leaders are born not made

Air Vice Marshal 'Johnny' Johnson was the top British Fighter Command ace pilot in the Second World War. In his biography *Wing Leader* (1956), Johnson recalls his sense of loss when the legendary Group Captain Douglas Bader was shot down over France.

'At Tangmere we had simply judged Bader on his ability as a leader and a fighter pilot, and for us the high sky would never be the same again. Gone was the confident, eager, often scornful voice. Exhorting us, sometimes cursing us, but always holding us together in the fight. Gone was the greatest tactician of them all. Today marked the end of an era that was rapidly becoming a legend.

The elusive, intangible qualities of leadership can never be taught, for a man either has them or he hasn't. Bader had them in full measure and on every flight had shown us how to apply them. He had taught us the true meaning of courage, spirit, determination, guts – call it what you will. Now that he was gone, it was our task to follow his signposts which pointed the way ahead.'

It would be wrong, however, to dismiss the qualities approach altogether. It was once the custom to do so among students of the subject. For example, C.A. Gibb, an influential American psychologist and editor of *Leadership: Selected Readings* (Penguin, 1969) could conclude: 'A leader is not a person characterized by any particular and consistent set of personality traits.'

In fact, contrary to this view we do now know some things about the personal qualities or characteristics that good leaders ought to and tend to possess. Although one cannot draw any hard-and-fast lines in this area, I make a rough working distinction between what could be called **representative** and **generic** qualities. The former are more rooted in a given working situation; the latter are found more widely across the board, in most leaders and at all times in history.

THE QUALITIES YOU NEED TO POSSESS

Let me begin with the **representative** qualities. Leaders tend to possess and exemplify the qualities expected or required in their working groups. Physical courage (which appears on most of the lists of military leadership) will not actually make you a leader in battle, but you cannot be one without it. If you aspire to be a sales manager, you should possess in large measure the qualities of a good salesperson. The head of an engineering department ought to exemplify the characteristics of an engineer, otherwise he or she will not gain and hold respect. Thus, a leader should mirror the group's characteristics. You cannot expect others to show qualities in their daily work – the compassion, kindness, warmth and courtesy of a good nurse, for example – if you as their leader do not show them yourself. It all comes back to leading by example. Do not be like the hypocrite who tells others to do what you don't practise yourself.

You can now see why leadership often springs from having a vocation or calling. That always lies in the field of human endeavour where your talents, interests, aptitudes and general personality find their optimum use in the service of others. It is the *good* nurse or the *good* scientist, for example, that enters the frame for being considered as a leader. Thus, as a corollary, it is important to find your true vocation – I suggest some ways to do that in *How to Find Your Vocation* (SCM Canterbury Press, 2000).

In that book, too, I sketched out the idea that leadership is really a 'second calling' – one that emerges out of one's original vocation in the fullness of time and one, incidentally, that may come to you as something of a surprise. So you do need to work hard in the early stages of your life to discover what the French call your *métier* – your true profession or trade.

How do you know that a person has found that natural centre? The poet W.H. Auden suggests a simple test:

> *You need not see what someone is doing*
> *To know if it is his vocation.*
> *You have only to watch his eyes:*
> *A cook making sauce, a surgeon*
> *Making a primary incision,*
> *A clerk completing a bill of lading,*
> *Wear the same rapt expression,*
> *Forgetting themselves in a function.*

What does your team read in your face each morning?

SOME GENERIC QUALITIES OF LEADERSHIP

The French author Marcel Proust once wrote: 'The writer, in order to attain generality and, so far as literature can, reality, needs to have seen many churches in order to paint one church, and for the portrayal of a single sentiment, he requires many individuals.'

I have been lucky over a long career to meet many leaders in many different fields, and I have heard or read about a legion of other ones too. Certain personal qualities have begun to stand out in my mind as being common, if not general or even universal. They are both qualities that effective leaders tend to have and qualities that – globally – people now look for in their leaders.

When the author John Buchan, then Governor-General of Canada, gave what I regard as a great lecture on the subject of leadership at the University of St Andrews in 1930, he offered his own list of leadership qualities but wisely added: 'We can make a list of the moral qualities of leaders but *not exhaust them*' (my italics). I agree with him. Therefore you should take the list that I offer you below as being indicative rather than exhaustive. It is open ended. You are free to add or subtract.

- Enthusiasm
- Integrity
- Toughness or demandingness and fairness
- Warmth and humanity
- Humility

EXERCISE 1: Leadership qualities
Before reading any further, take a piece of paper and write across the top the names of two individuals known

to you personally whom you regard as leaders. See if you can explore the above qualities in them by giving them a mark out of ten for each quality. Can you think of some episode where a particular quality was exemplified?

Here are a few notes on each of the generic qualities that have emerged from the sieve of my own mind. Please add any additional thoughts or comments that occur to you.

Enthusiasm

Can you think of any leader worthy of the name who lacks enthusiasm? Certainly I can't. That is why it is top of my generic qualities list.

For the Greeks, enthusiasm was a divine gift. The Greek word literally means to be possessed by a god – what we would now call to be inspired. The symptoms of an enthusiastic person are well known: a lively or strong interest for a cause of activity; a great eagerness; an intense and sometimes even a passionate zeal for the work in hand. You can see why Shakespeare in *Henry IV* identifies enthusiasm as 'the very lifeblood of our enterprise'. It is the lifeblood of your enterprise too.

Integrity

Hard on the heels of enthusiasm comes integrity. I referred to it in my first lecture on leadership, 'Leadership in History', when I was in the sixth form at school and since then I have never once spoken on leadership without mentioning integrity.

Field Marshal Lord Slim once defined integrity to me as 'the quality which makes people trust you'. Mutual trust between the leader and the led is absolutely vital: lose that and you have lost everything. Moreover, it is very hard to re-establish it. As the Roman historian Livy said, 'Trust being lost, all the social intercourse of men is brought to nothing.'

Integrity, from the Latin *integer*, literally means wholeness: an integer is a whole number. But with reference to people it signifies the trait that comes from a loyal adherence to values or standards *outside yourself*, especially the truth: it is a wholeness which stems from being true to truth. We know what it means when people say of a scholar or artist that he or she has integrity. They do not deceive themselves or other people. They are not manipulators. As Oliver Cromwell once wrote in a letter to a friend: 'Subtlety may deceive you, integrity never will.'

Just why it is that people who have integrity in this sense creates trust in others I shall leave you to reflect upon at your leisure. Certainly we all know that a person who deliberately misleads us by telling lies sooner or later forfeits our trust.

There are situations in life which can test your integrity, sometimes to the uttermost. A person of integrity comes through such trials, tests and temptations. Rudyard Kipling writes of such personal moral victory in his poem *If*, which lightly sketches integrity in outline.

> *If you can keep your head when all about you*
> *Are losing theirs and blaming it on you.*
> *If you can trust yourself when all men doubt you,*
> *But make allowance for their doubting too;*
>
> *If you can wait and not be tired of waiting,*
> *Or being lied about, don't deal in lies,*
> *Or being hated, don't give way to hating,*
> *And yet don't look too good, nor talk too wise . . .*

Toughness or demandingness and fairness

As a leader you need to be tough or demanding but fair. Leadership is not being popular; it is not about wanting to be liked by everyone. For leaders make demands, they set high standards, and they will not accept anything but the best. That isn't always popular.

> The great conductor Otto Klemperer expected the best from his players and didn't go into raptures when he got it. After one performance, however, he was so pleased with the orchestra that he looked at them and said, 'Good!' Overwhelmed, the musicians burst into applause. 'Not *that* good,' Klemperer said.

As Confucius commented long ago, 'The best leader is easy to serve and difficult to please.' Notice that where praise is given sparingly it is valued more.

Toughness is indicative of more than being demanding in terms of the common task. Akin to resilience and firmness, it is the quality that enables you to withstand tension, strain or stress. To be firm means being fixed and unshakeable, and often implies deep commitment to a moral principle. People look for this particular form of strength in a leader. As one Arab proverb puts it, 'No strength within, no respect without.' St Augustine once prayed for a 'heart of fire' for humanity's common purpose, a 'heart of love' to others, and to himself a 'heart of steel'. All true leaders have that steel in their souls.

Personally I hate war, but it is undeniable that we have learnt a great deal about leadership by the experience of battle. Such crisis situations, where life and death are at stake – viewed over three thousand years and in every part of the world – are revealing about human nature, especially about what kind of leadership elicits the best response. What is evident is that soldiers respond best to leaders who are neither harsh nor soft.

The leader who liked to be liked and the commander who was not a leader

The classic description of these types of leadership comes in Xenophon's account of a military expedition of some 10,000 Greek mercenary soldiers who fought on one side in a Persian civil war and then made a famous 800 miles march through what is now Iraq and Turkey to freedom. Xenophon, who had studied leadership with Socrates and later wrote the world's first books on leadership, served on the campaign as a cavalry commander. Unsurprisingly, given the influence of Socrates as a teacher, Xenophon was an acute observer of the leadership abilities of the Greek generals.

Proxenus of the city of Boeotia was a very ambitious and well-educated young man who joined the Greek mercenary army in Persia in 40 BC. He was in search of fame and fortune. Though without any practical military experience – he had been tutored by an academic in military tactics – he secured office through his political contacts as one of the expedition's six generals. Xenophon, who was invited by Proxenus to join the expedition to Persia, has left us this pen portrait of his friend and companion:

'He was a good commander for people of a gentlemanly type, but he was not capable of impressing his soldiers with a feeling of respect or fear for him. Indeed he showed more diffidence in front of his soldiers than his subordinates showed in front of him, and it was obvious that he was more afraid of being unpopular with his troops than his troops were afraid of disobeying his orders.'

Xenophon has also left us a pen portrait of the veteran Spartan general Clearchus. In the crisis that followed the defeat of their patrons in the battle of Cunaxe outside Babylon, when the Greeks were faced with a choice between slavery or a long, hazardous march through enemy-occupied territory to the Black Sea and freedom, it was to Clearchus that everyone looked – for he had that inner steel as well as the experience of having been in such situation before. He knew what to do. Yet Xenophon describes him as a harsh man; except when an army was in a crisis no one would voluntarily choose to serve with him. In other words, he was a commander but not a leader.

In the event, by an act of treachery, the Persians assassinated all the Greek generals and Xenophon, aged twenty-six, was among the six elected by the soldiers to replace them. Needless to say, Xenophon aspired – not without some success – to be a great military leader.

Toughness and demandingness should always be expressed in the context of fairness: a true leader has no favourites. A former Royal Navy captain put it like this:

> Make demands, but not unreasonably so. Leaders need to be even-handed in their demands on subordinates. Those in the navy who demanded too much of their immediate subordinates – typically heads-of-department – generated a negative, joyless atmosphere: but those who were soft on these people would lose their community's respect. Consistency was profoundly important, not least in the handling of discipline. The Captain has to discipline proven offenders under naval law and regulation, knowing that the person (unless the offence is gross) continues as an essential working member of the warship community. Sailors understand well this need for good order: harshness will disturb them, but so will inconsistency or inappropriate leniency.

EXERCISE 2: Have you got what it takes for a top job in leadership?

Place the following attributes in order of 'most valuable at the top level of leadership' by placing a number 1 to 25 beside them. This exercise can be done by you individually, or with others in a group.

- Ambition
- Willingness to work hard
- Enterprise
- Astuteness
- Ability to 'stick to it'
- Capacity for lucid writing
- Imagination
- Ability to spot opportunities
- Willingness to work long hours
- Curiosity
- Understanding of others
- Skill with numbers
- Capacity for abstract thought
- Integrity
- Ability to administer efficiently
- Enthusiasm
- Capacity to speak lucidly
- Single-mindedness
- Willingness to take risks
- Leadership
- Ability to take decisions
- Analytical ability
- Ability to meet unpleasant situations
- Open-mindedness
- Ability to adapt quickly to change

Now turn to page 220 and compare your answers with the ratings given to these attributes by a cross section of successful chief executives.

Warmth and humanity

As a general principle, a 'cold fish' – meaning a totally unemotional or impassive person – does not make a good leader. For in all personal relations, be they professional or private, people do not respond well to a perceived or actual coldness in others. As the Chinese proverb puts it,

'You can live with cold tea and cold rice but not with cold words.'

A warmth of feeling, a general friendliness of attitude, and an unobtrusive solicitude for the welfare of individuals are all hallmarks of the good leader. Empathy is the power of entering into another's mind and imaginatively experiencing (and so fully comprehending) the way things are for that person. Empathy, however, should lead to acts that show that you care. Caring here means taking seriously the welfare of others – your colleagues or companions in the common enterprise. Put their needs before your own.

Marcus Aurelius, Roman emperor from AD 160 to 180, was a world leader of his day. He was burdened with a great responsibility. For much of his reign he led his legions against the Germanic tribes, who were invading the Roman empire from the north. By nature he was a reflective thinker; a lover of practical wisdom. His *Meditations* are still a classic: a collection of aphorisms and reflections written down as much for his own guidance as a leader as a book for others. Speaking to himself – and yet to all leaders – he writes: 'Love those people heartily that it is your fortune to be engaged with.'

Humility

In the context of leadership **humility** is best understood as the lack of arrogance. Arrogance is not an attractive attribute in anyone, let alone a leader.

Willingness to own up to one's own mistakes or errors of judgement rather than to make others into scapegoats is one hallmark of humility. Domineering, over-assertive or tyrannical men or women don't do that – they are always right even when their ship is sinking. Another important characteristic is open-mindedness to those views and opinions of others that challenge your own ideas or assumptions. Lastly, the ability to continue to learn, change and grow until the end of your days is the blessing that humility – not the easiest yoke – will confer on you.

Any form of play-acting or hypocrisy is incompatible with humility. That is why a humble person never pretends to be better or worse, more important or less important than they really are. As Dag Hammarskjöld wrote: 'Humility is just as much the opposite of self-abasement as it is of self-exaltation.'

SUMMARY

> *I cannot hear what you are saying;*
> *What you are is shouting at me.*

This Zulu proverb reminds us of the importance of personality and character in leadership.

Representative qualities are those which are expected or required in your working group: you should aim to exemplify them.

Generic qualities are found across the board. They give a 'family likeness' to all effective leaders, whatever their level, field or cultural background. Humanity knows what it expects in its leaders. Enthusiasm, integrity, toughness or demandingness, fairness, warmth, humanity and humility are the commonly found moral characteristics of effective leaders. This list, however, is indicative rather than exhaustive. Therefore, while an understanding of leadership in terms of the qualities of character which one person has to a greater degree than his or her fellows is relevant, it is far from being the whole story.

> *You are not born a leader, you become one.*
> A proverb of the Bambileke people
> in West Africa

CHECKLIST:
DO YOU HAVE SOME BASIC LEADERSHIP QUALITIES?

List the five key characteristics or personal qualities which are expected or required in workers in your field.

Now rate yourself in terms of each of them – Good, Average or Weak.

	Good	Average	Weak
_____	☐	☐	☐
_____	☐	☐	☐
_____	☐	☐	☐
_____	☐	☐	☐
_____	☐	☐	☐

Circle the number where you would place yourself on the following continuum:

VERY INTROVERT								VERY EXTROVERT
5	4	3	2	1	2	3	4	5

(Leaders tend to be slightly more extrovert than introvert on this scale, i.e. they are ambiverts – mixtures of both)

	Yes	No
Have you shown yourself to be a responsible person?	☐	☐
Do you like the responsibility as well as the rewards of leadership?	☐	☐

Are you self-sufficient enough to withstand criticism, indifference or unpopularity from others and to work effectively with others without constant supervision? ☐ ☐

Are you an active and socially participative person? ☐ ☐

Can you control your emotions and moods – or do they control you? ☐ ☐

Have you any evidence to suppose that other people think of you as essentially a warm person? ☐ ☐

Can you give instances over the past three months where you have been deliberately dishonest or less than straight with the people that work for you? ☐ ☐

Are you noted for your enthusiasm at work? ☐ ☐

Has anyone ever used the word 'integrity' in relation to you? ☐ ☐

2

WHAT YOU HAVE TO KNOW OR LEARN

'There is a small risk that leaders will be
regarded with contempt by those they lead if
whatever they ask of others they show themselves
best able to perform.'

Xenophon

The second main approach to understanding leadership
focuses upon the **situation.** Taken to extremes, this school
declares there is no such thing as a born leader: it all
depends upon the situation. Some situations will evoke
leadership from one person, others will bring it out in
another – therefore it is useless discussing leadership in
general terms. This 'situational approach', as it is called,
holds that it is always the situation which determines who
emerges as the leader and what 'style of leadership' he or
she has to adopt. Who becomes a leader of a particular
group engaging in a particular activity, and what the characteristics are in the given case, are a function of the specific
situation.

To illustrate this theory, let us imagine some survivors of

a shipwreck landing on a tropical island. The soldier in theparty might take command if natives attacked them, thebuilder might organize the work of erecting houses, and the farmer might direct the labour of growing food. In other words, leadership would pass from member to member according to the situation. Note that 'situation' in this context means primarily the task of the group. If an airliner crashes in a jungle the person who takes command for the survival operation might not be the captain of the aircraft but the person most qualified for the job. Change the situation, and you change the leader.

THE THREE KINDS OF AUTHORITY AT WORK

This 'horses for courses' approach has some obvious advantages. It emphasizes the importance of *knowledge* relevant to a specific problem situation – 'authority flows to the one who knows', as one writer put it. There are broadly three kinds of authority at work:

- the authority of **position** – job title, badges of rank, appointment
- the authority of **personality** – the natural qualities of influence
- the authority of **knowledge** – technical, professional.

Whereas leaders in the past tended to rely upon the first kind of authority – that is, they exercised mastery as the appointed boss – today leaders have to draw much more upon the second and third kinds of authority.

KENT: You have a look upon your face that I would fain call master.

KING LEAR: What is that?
KENT: Authority.

                                        Shakespeare, *King Lear*

But technical knowledge is not everything. It is especially important in the early stages of your career, when people tend to be specialists. As your career broadens out, however, more general skills – such as leadership, communication and decision making – come into their own. You need to acquire these general skills, for technical knowledge alone will not make you into a leader.

Michael, aged 36 years, had a brilliant career as a 'back-room boy' in the accounts department of a British pharmaceutical company. He had passed all the examinations and specialized in tax matters, winning himself a solid reputation. He had been with the same firm for twelve years. On 'situational' grounds he was the ideal man to become the leader of his department when the job fell vacant. When that promotion came his way, however, it took him by surprise. He was not prepared for leadership. The company was in recession; morale in the department was low. He soon found himself faced with all sorts of problems, both about the department's effectiveness and about people, where his expertise in tax law was of no help. He floundered for a while and then in desperation left the company to set up business on his own as a tax consultant.

How far are the general skills of leadership transferable from one working situation to another? The skills are certainly transferable, but often the people are not. One reason may be that the people concerned do not have the technical or professional knowledge required for another field. Like courage in the case of the soldier, such knowledge and experience does not make you into a leader, but you cannot be one without it. That does not mean that leaders cannot change fields (e.g. industry for politics) as opposed to making major changes within fields (e.g. becoming managing director of an electronic company after running a car assembly plant) – but it implies that they will not be successful unless they can quickly learn the essentials or principles of the new industry or occupation.

Within a given field, such as a manufacturing industry, there are other situational determinants besides the type of produce. Size – small, medium or large – is one factor in the equation. Some industrial leaders are attracted naturally to situations where a company needs 'turning around' after a story of decline and loss of morale. Others prefer a lively, technologically advanced company going for rapid growth.

Socrates on leadership

The first person to teach what is now called the situational approach – that 'authority flows to the one who knows' – was none other than Socrates in ancient Athens. Socrates himself wrote no books, but two of his students, Plato and Xenophon, published books in the form of dialogues between Socrates and various interlocutors. How far these dialogues were remembered conversations or independent creative works is hard to assess, but the original inspiration of Socrates is undeniable.

In this context Xenophon and Plato, quite independently, give us the same illustrative example or parable about leadership, in both cases attributed to Socrates. The following is Plato's version. (To understand this extract it is useful to know that in Greek times the helmsman of a ship – the *kubernator*, whence our word *governor* – was also usually both the navigator and ship's captain.)

'The sailors are quarrelling over control of the helm ...

They do not understand that the genuine navigator can only make himself fit to command a ship by studying the seasons of the year, sky, stars and winds, and all that belongs to his craft; and they have no idea that, along with the science of navigation, it is possible for him to gain by instruction or practice, the skill to keep control of the helm whether some like it or not.'

'Have you not noticed', Socrates asked a young man who came to him in the hope of learning how to become a leader, 'that no incompetent person ever attempts to exercise authority over our harpists, choristers and dancers, nor over wrestlers? *All who have authority over them can tell you where they learned their business.*'

Incidentally, Socrates also taught that where women know more than men (in the professional or technical sense) they will tend to be accepted as leaders. He gave the weaving industry in Athens as a good example.

THE NEED FOR FLEXIBILITY

Even within a given field – or within a particular organization within it – the situation varies. Some people argue that such changes require a change of leader. A company in growth may need a bustling, entrepreneurial leader, but once it has established its produce lines and market share that person may get frustrated and should be replaced by a different sort of person.

A chemical company on Teesside set up a new plant to make ammonia. During the commissioning phase, which lasted several years, there were many crises. The plant frequently broke down; there were accidents and all sorts of 'bugs' in the system. Eventually the plant was fully 'on stream'. In the new 'steady state' the first manager, who thrived on technical challenges, became inappropriate. He was replaced by a less abrasive person who devoted far more time to developing good working relationships, which is what the new situation now required.

The answer, of course, is to develop as much *flexibility* as you can within your limitations. However, it is always hard to know what those limitations are. It is easy to make assumptions about them which turn out to be unfounded.

Mark never thought of himself as a leader in a crisis. He worked as a school teacher in South London. One holiday he took a party of boys and girls hill walking in Wales. One evening, a boy who disobeyed instructions and wandered off on his own fell down a disused mineshaft. Far from panicking, Mark found himself becoming calmer. He took charge of the situation. After the rescue services arrived and had extricated the boy, they congratulated Mark on the leadership he had shown. He was completely exhausted, but he had learnt an important truth about himself. Contrary to his expectations and those of his colleagues, he had revealed the ability to respond to and lead in a crisis. By chance a similar but more serious accident took place in Italy that year, when a small boy got stuck down a narrow well-shaft. Complete chaos reigned. Even the President of Italy, who hastened to the scene, could not give the necessary leadership, and the child died.

Most people discover as they grow older that they are more suited in terms of their aptitudes, interests and temperament to lead in some fields rather than others. Some characteristic working situations, for example, call for speed of reaction or swift apprehension.

Some contingencies cannot be foreseen. War provides

plenty of examples of such occasions when quickness of thought is essential for success. In conversation with Las Casas one day, Napoleon reflected on the rarity of this ability to react swiftly in sudden emergencies: 'As to moral courage, I have rarely met with the *two-o'clock-in-the-morning* kind: I mean unprepared courage, that which is necessary on an unexpected occasion; and which, in spite of the most unforeseen events, leaves full freedom of judgement and decision.'

No victim of false modesty, Napoleon did not hesitate to say that he was himself eminently endowed with this 'two-o'clock-in-the-morning' courage, and that he had met few persons equal to himself in this respect.

A major implication of the situational approach, as I have already suggested, is that you should select the field in which you wish to exercise leadership with care. Usually interests, aptitude and temperament are sufficiently good guides. With my poor aptitude for music, for example, I should be wasting my time to aspire to conduct the Vienna Symphony Orchestra. Once you have chosen your field, however, you should aim to develop maximum *flexibility* within it, so that you are the master at reading the changes in situations and responding with the appropriate leadership style. At the same time as you are growing in leadership, your technical knowledge and experience in that working field should be widening and deepening as well.

Know your field of activity

Another quality common to leaders is their willingness to work hard, to prepare themselves, to know their field of activity thoroughly. I have often heard it said of some individual: 'Oh, he'll get by on his personality.' Well, he may 'get by' for a time but if a charming personality is all he has, the day will come when he will find himself looking for a job.

I never knew President Roosevelt as well as I did some of the other world leaders, but in the few conferences I had with him I was impressed, not only by his inspirational qualities, but by his amazing grasp of the whole complex war effort. He could discuss strategy on equal terms with his generals and admirals. His knowledge of the geography of the war theatres was so encyclopaedic that the most obscure places in faraway countries were always accurately sited on his mental map. President Roosevelt possessed personality, but as his nation's leader in a global conflict, he also did his homework – thoroughly.

Dwight D. Eisenhower

SUMMARY

'Let each man pass his days in that wherein his skill is greatest,' wrote the Roman poet Propertius in the first century BC. As a leader, you should have the kind of temperament, personal qualities and knowledge required by the working **situation** you have chosen.

Technical competence or professional knowledge is a key strand in your authority. Yet expertise in a particular job is not enough; other more general skills are also required. These focus upon leadership, decision making and communication. These can be **transferred** as you move into a different situation in your field or change to a new sphere of work.

Within your field you should aim to widen your knowledge of the work and develop the general abilities of leading others. That will increase your **flexibility**. Even within the broad continuities of a particular industry or business, *the situation will change*. Social, technical or economic developments will see to that. Are you ready?

The authority of position remains important. But a mountaineer climbing in the Himalayas does not entrust his life to a single strand of rope. You need to weave together all three strands of authority – position, personality and knowledge – if you want to have the natural authority of a good leader.

CHECKLIST:
ARE YOU RIGHT FOR THE SITUATION?

	Yes	No
Do you feel that your interests, aptitudes (e.g. mechanical, verbal) and temperament are suited to the field you are in?	☐	☐
Can you identify a field where you would be more likely to emerge as a leader?	☐	☐
How have you developed 'the authority of knowledge'?	☐	☐
Have you done all you can at this stage in your career to acquire the necessary professional or specialist training available?	☐	☐
Do you have experience in more than one field or more than one industry of more than one function?	☐	☐
Do you take an interest in fields adjacent to your own and potentially relevant?	☐	☐

Sometimes ☐

Never ☐

Always ☐

How flexible are you within your field? Are you:

Good   You have responded to situational changes ☐
with marked flexibility or approach; you read
situations well, think about them and respond
with the appropriate kind of leadership.

Adequate   You have proved yourself in two
             situations, but you fear some situations;
             you are happiest only when the situation
             is normal and predictable.   □

Weak   You are highly adapted to one particular
             work environment and cannot stand
             change. You are often called rigid or
             inflexible.   □

3

WHAT YOU HAVE TO DO

*'Not the cry but the flight of the wild duck
leads the flock to fly and follow.'*
Chinese proverb

A third line of thinking and research about leadership focuses on the group. This 'group approach' tends to see leadership in terms of functions which meet group needs: what has to be *done*. In fact, if you look closely at matters involving leadership, there are always three elements or variables:

- The **leader** – qualities of personality and character
- The **situation** – partly constant, partly varying
- The **group** – the followers: their needs and values.

GROUP PERSONALITY AND GROUP NEEDS

Working groups are, according to my theory, more than the sum of their parts: they have a life and identity of their own. All such groups, providing they have been together for a certain amount of time, develop their own unique ethos. I call this phenomenon **group personality** – a phrase borrowed from a British prime minister, Clement Attlee.

Group personality

It is more important that the Cabinet discussion should take place, so to speak, at a higher level than the information and opinions provided by the various departmental briefs. A collection of departmental Ministers does not make a Cabinet. A Cabinet consists only of responsible human beings. And it is their thinking and judgement in broad terms that make a Government tick, not arguments about the recommendations of civil servants. It is interesting to note that quite soon a Cabinet begins to develop a group personality. The role of the Prime Minister is to cultivate this, if it is efficient and right-minded; to do his best to modify it, if it is not.

While a collection of departmental heads mouthing their top civil servants' briefs is unsatisfactory, a collection of Ministers who are out of touch with the administration tends to be unrealistic. And a Minister who has an itch to run everybody else's department as well as, or in preference to, his own is just a nuisance. Some men will be ready to express a view about everything. They should be discouraged. If necessary, I would shut them up. Once is enough.

Clement Attlee

In practice, the phenomenon of group personality means that what works in one group may not work in its apparent twin group within the same organization.

James Rivers managed a branch of one of the high-street banks in the North of England for five years. He introduced several ideas, most noticeably more social activities for the staff: dances, theatre outings and competitions.

These were warmly welcomed, and James was asked several times to talk about the successful effect of these innovations on staff morale. When he was appointed manager of another branch the same size in London he eagerly arranged a similar programme, but it attracted no support. Rivers also noticed that many of his favourite sayings and ideas also fell flat on their faces. He felt somewhat exasperated. 'The whole atmosphere is so different,' he groaned to his area manager. 'It's as if I have moved to a foreign country! You wouldn't think it was the same company.'

In order for such a corporate personality to emerge, of course, a group has to be in the formative stage for some time. Then its unique character becomes apparent. It acquires something like a collective memory. Especially when groups are in their formative stages, leaders can do a great deal to set the tone of this distinctive nature.

The other half of the theory stresses **what groups share in common** as compared with their uniqueness. They are analogous to individuals in this respect: different as we are in terms of appearance and personality, we share in common our needs – at midnight all of us usually begin to feel tired; at breakfast time we shall be hungry, and so on. According to my model, there are three areas of need present in working groups:

1. To achieve the **common task**
2. To be held together or to **maintain itself as a cohesive unity**
3. The **needs** which **each individual brings** with them into the group.

TASK NEEDS

One of the reasons why a group comes together is that there is a task which one person cannot do on their own. But does the group as a whole experience the need to complete the task within the natural time limits for it? A human being is not very aware of a need for food if they are already well fed, and so one would expect a group to be relatively oblivious of any sense of need if its task is being successfully performed. In this case the only sign of a need having been met is the satisfaction or elation which overtakes the group in its moments of triumph – a happiness which as social beings we count among our deepest joys.

Before such a fulfilment, however, many groups pass through a 'black night of despair' when it may appear that the group will be compelled to disperse without achieving what it set out to do. If the members are not committed to the common goal this will be a comparatively painless event, but if they are, the group will exhibit various degrees of anxiety and frustration. Scapegoats for the corporate failure may be chosen and punished; reorganizations might take place and new leaders emerge. Thus, adversity reveals the nature of group life more clearly than prosperity. In it we may see signs or symptoms of the need to get on effectively with whatever the group has come together to do.

GROUP MAINTENANCE NEEDS

This is not so easy to perceive as the task need: as with an iceberg, much of the life of any group lies below the surface. The distinction that the task need concerns things while the group maintenance need involves people does not help much. Again, it helps to think of groups which are threatened – from without by forces aimed at their disintegration or from within by disruptive people or ideas. We can then see how they give priority to maintaining themselves against these external or internal pressures, sometimes showing great ingenuity in the process.

Many of the written or unwritten rules of the group are designed to promote this unity and to maintain cohesiveness at all costs. Those who rock the boat, or infringe group standards and corporate balance, may expect reactions varying from friendly indulgence to downright anger. Instinctively, a common feeling exists that 'united we stand, divided we fall'; that good relationships, desirable in themselves, are also an essential means towards the shared end. This need to create and promote group cohesiveness I call the team maintenance need.

I decided to replace the term 'group maintenance' with 'team maintenance' when the time came to apply theory to training leaders. It sounded just a little less like jargon. The earliest teams in the ancient language of England were sets of draught animals pulling together. Today, of course, a 'team' is our most common word for a group of people who form a side in a game or sport. So today everyone knows what a team is. The words 'group' and 'team' are not exact synonyms; all teams are groups, but not all groups are teams.

In the context of work today, 'team' is a better word than 'group'. For the key characteristic of a team is *differentiation of roles in relation to a common goal*. The functions of the football goalkeeper, for example, differ from those of the full backs or midfield players, yet all eleven members of the team, whatever their roles, share a common purpose and a common goal.

INDIVIDUAL NEEDS

Thirdly, individuals bring into the group their own needs – not just the physical ones for food and shelter, which are largely catered for by the payment of wages these days, but also their psychological needs: recognition, a sense of doing something worthwhile; status; the deeper needs to give to and receive from other people in a working situation. These personal needs are perhaps more profound than we sometimes realize.

These needs spring from the depths of our common life as human beings. They may attract us to – or repel us from – any given group. Underlying them all is the fact that people need each other, not just to survive but to achieve and develop personality. As the African proverb says, 'It takes a whole village to grow a person.' This growth occurs in a whole range of social activities – friendship, marriage, neighbourhood – but inevitably work groups are extremely important because so many people spend so much of their waking time in them.

It is worth reflecting for a moment on the importance of that distinction between *group* and *individual*, as opposed to allowing them to be blurred together as *people* or 'human relations' or (even worse!) the 'socio-emotional area'. Of course, individuality and individualism can be taken too far. For, as indicated above, we do not become *persons* except in relation to others. In some cultures at certain times there has been a tendency to subordinate the individual to the group. The implicit message was that groups are stronger, wiser and sometimes even more creative than the individuals in it. 'What the group wants' became the ultimate court of appeal. Although there are cultural differences of emphasis, however, leaders should always be aware of both the **group** and each **individual**, and seek to harmonise them in the service of the third factor – the **common task**.

Understanding the individual

Individual needs are especially important in relation to motivation, which is closely connected with leadership. One of the things that leaders are supposed to do is to motivate people by a combination of rewards and threats – the carrot-and-stick approach. Yet, according to another body of theory, you and I motivate ourselves to a large extent by responding to inner needs. As a leader you must understand these needs in individuals and how they operate, so that you can work with the grain of human nature and not against it.

In this field, as in the others, it is useful for you to have a 'sketch map'. Here, A.H. Maslow's concept of a 'hierarchy of needs' is still valuable. He suggested that individual needs are arranged in an order – from the stronger to the weaker (but more distinctively human). These needs are often shown in a pyramid model, but actually Maslow did not present them in a visual model. Here is my own framework for representing them.

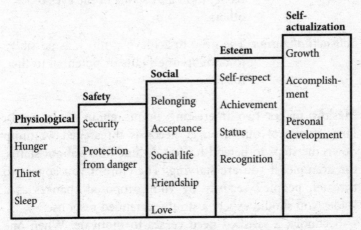

Maslow's hierarchy of needs

Physiological   These are humanity's physical needs for food, shelter, warmth, sexual gratification and other bodily functions.

Safety   These include the need to feel safe from physical danger and the need for physical, mental and emotional security.

Social   This covers the need for belonging and love, the need to feel part of a group or organization; to belong to or be with someone else. Implicit in it is the need to give and receive love; to share and to be part of a family.

Esteem   These needs fall into two closely related categories – self-esteem and the esteem of others. The first includes our need to respect ourselves; to feel personal worth, adequacy and competence. The second embraces our need for respect, praise, recognition and status in the eyes of others.

Self-actualization The need to achieve as much as possible; to develop one's gifts or potential to the full.

Maslow makes two interesting points about these needs. First, if one of our stronger needs is threatened we jump down the steps to defend it. You do not worry about status, for example, if you are starving. Therefore if you appear to threaten people's security by your proposed changes as a leader you should expect a stoutly defended response.

Secondly, a satisfied need ceases to motivate. When one area of need is met, the person concerned becomes aware of another set of needs within him or her. These in turn now begin to be the motivating force. There is obviously much in this theory – when the physiological and security needs in particular have been satisfied they do not move us so strongly. How far this principle extends up the scale is a matter for discussion.

Elsewhere in his work Maslow postulated other hierarchies of need, which he had identified 'like galaxies in the vast reaches of the unconscious mind': *cognitive needs* (curiosity, the need to find out and to understand) and *aesthetic needs* (the need for beauty, order and elegance). In his later life he also talked much about what could be called *spiritual needs*, the need to escape from oneself and to feel part of some larger transcendent unity above the self. As a secular human-ist, Maslow did not give the name God to this welcoming Other in which self is both lost and found, but the influence of the Jewish tradition in which he was reared is clearly evident.

Maslow made another significant contribution to under-standing individual needs by reiterating the distinction between **instrumental** and **expressive** behaviour. Much of what we do is to meet our needs: it is a means or instrument towards an end. But a person also does or says things to express what he or she is or has become. A skater or a dancer, for instance, is expressing themselves. This percep-tion can help us to understand why others are doing things. You could also look on leadership as both instrumental – a means of meeting task, team and individual needs – and also expressive of all that you are and can become in terms of personality, character and skill.

THE THREE CIRCLES MODEL

The next major step, as I described it in *Training for Leadership* (McDonald and Jane's, 1968), is to relate the three areas of need together in the Three Circles model, below.

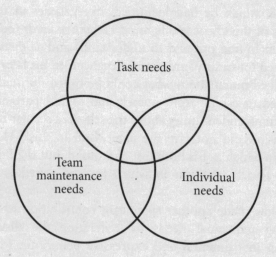

Mathematicians will recognize this framework as a Venn diagram. It was so named after the English logician John Venn (1834–1923), who first used the circular intersecting areas to represent mathematical sets and show the relations between them.

The interaction of needs

The Three Circles model suggests quite simply that the task, team and individual needs are always interacting with each other. The circles overlap but they do not sit on top of each other. In other words, there is always some degree of tension between them. Many of an individual's needs – such as the need to achieve and the social need for human companionship – are met in part by participating in working groups. But an individual can also run the risk of being exploited in the interests of the task and dominated by the group in ways that trespass upon one's personal freedom and integrity.

It is a fundamental feature of the Three Circles model that each of the circles must always be seen in relation to the other two. As a leader you need to be constantly aware of what is happening in your group in terms of the three circles. You might imagine one circle as a balloon getting bigger (better) and another shrinking, or you may visualize the situation as if one circle is completely eclipsed or blacked out.

EXERCISE 3: The Three Circles model 1
Cut a disc or use a round lid to cover one circle in the model. At once, segments of the other two circles are covered also. Using the disc and doing the following exercise you can begin to develop this awareness of the interrelationship between the circles yourself.

1. Cover the task circle with the disc.
   If a team fails in its task this will intensify the disintegrative tendencies present in the team and diminish the satisfaction of individual needs.

   Polymotors, an engineering company employing fifty people, consistently failed to fill its order books after a change of management. The sales manager blamed the production head, and vice versa. They stopped talking to each other. Morale slumped. Some individuals left in disgust. Eventually the firm failed and all 50 lost their jobs in a time of high unemployment.

   Can you think of another example from your experience?

2. Cover the **team circle** with the disc.
   If there is a lack of unity or harmonious relationships in the team this will affect performance on the job and also individual needs.

   The Research and Development department in a large electronics firm based in Boston, USA, fell victim to team disunity. Clashes of personality and rival cliques made daily work a nightmare. Through poor internal communication the team failed to meet work deadlines. The creativity of the team dropped to zero. Absentee-ism soon increased as individuals found their social needs totally frustrated at work. Eventually the depart-ment had to be divided between two others.

Can you add a further example from your experience?

3. Cover the **individual circle** with the disc.
   If an individual feels frustrated and unhappy, he or she will not make their maximum contribution to either the common task or to the life of the team.

   Henry worked in a city law office. He had been there for more than twenty years and was taken for granted. No one bothered to explain the firm's progress or pros-pects to him. He felt he should have been promoted some years before, but when a job became available it was given to a younger man. Henry also felt bored and frustrated because his suggestions for improving work procedures had been ignored. Gradually he withdrew into his shell. He gave the minimum effort to his work and insisted on leaving the office promptly at 5 p.m. He no longer shared his lunch break with his colleagues. 'I am just waiting for retirement,' he said to me. But retire-ment was ten years away!

Can you think of another example?

Each individual has a piece of social power. That means that he or she can help to build up good relationships and a positive climate at work. On the other hand an individual person can, by ignorance or design, use his or her influence in a negative way. Hostile or damaging gossip behind people's backs, for example, eats away relationships in the long run as surely as acid dripping onto metal. Gossip as such is an aspect of our interest in people and human nature, and it is mostly harmless. But vicious and unfounded gossip corrodes trust at work. A positive individual may serve the team by challenging the gossipers or the bullies. You do not have to be the leader to do that.

The three circles in the model will also affect each other if there is a *positive* change in any one of them.

- Achievement in terms of a **common aim** tends to build a sense of **team identity** – the 'we-feeling', as some have called it. The moment of victory closes the psychological gaps between people: morale rises naturally.
- **Good internal communications** and a **developed team spirit** based upon past successes make a team much more likely to do well in its **task area**, and incidentally provide a more satisfactory climate for the individual.
- An **individual whose needs are recognized** and who feels that he or she can make a characteristic and worthwhile **contribution both to the task and the team** will tend to produce good fruits in both these areas.

The following case study comes from my own experience. During my National Service I found myself in charge of a platoon of Scots Guardsmen in the Canal Zone of Egypt. We were part of the forces guarding the Suez Canal, which meant for us various guard duties in the vicinity of Port Said. For six months or more the platoon was split up in this way, coming together only for drill or administration. In the summer the whole battalion moved south to guard a vast ammunition dump in the flat desert waste. My platoon was given the job of laying a thick and broad wire barrier around a section of this place. We had to drive out to the place in a lorry with all the supplies, and then start work where our predecessors had left off. The dump was so large that we were almost out of sight of any buildings.

On the first day we laid about 200 yards of wire. It was extremely hot and the soldiers did not look especially happy. Next day I took my shirt off and worked with the men, twisting wire and knocking in stakes. By teatime we had put down 300 yards of entanglements. That evening I worked out several ways of doing the job faster, such as dumping stores in advance of the work, and again next day we laid more wire. By the fourth day a remarkable change had come over the platoon: they were cheerful, keen, full of ideas, reluctant to stop work and eager to set a higher target for the fifth day. So it continued for ten days.

I noticed a big change in Guardsman McCluskey, a real troublemaker back in barracks. Here he emerged as a leader of a subgroup. He was enthusiastically still talking about ways of laying more wire if we could be allowed to obtain certain other types of equipment when the time came to hand over the job to the next platoon. 'You'll never lay 700 yards of wire in a day like *we* have done,' announced McCluskey to the newcomers. Nor did they! Although I carried the scars of the barbed wire on my arms for several years, I looked back upon those days under the burning sun as not only happy ones, but also as extremely significant for my understanding of leadership.

Incidentally, I had much the same job to do with Bedouin soldiers when I was in the Arab Legion, this time under more hazardous conditions. The Bedouins responded just as well. As Lawrence of Arabia said, 'The Bedouins are hard to drive but easy to lead.' Aren't we all?

EXERCISE 4: The Three Circles model

1. Can you give an example from your experience where the team circle has been exceptionally good – real team spirit, plenty of synergy, excellent personal relations and good communication – enabling the team to deal positively with task factors that would have defeated a less capable group? What have been the effects of such a team on the individual within it? – think of a particular case known to you.

   Techcom, a small firm of 150 people, had built up excellent working relations and morale was extremely high. Management and employees trusted each other and liked working together; they believed in the future of their industry and wanted to expand. Then they were hit by a downturn in the domestic market and some fierce competition from China, India and Korea. The employees volunteered to take a cut in their wages; the management promised there would be no redundancies if they could help it. Everyone redoubled their efforts. Soon business improved again and they were back in profit.

2. Add now an example where an individual has effectively influenced the task circle and also benefited the team as a whole.

   Outstanding examples of the influence of the individual on the other two circles are often provided by two kinds of members – *leaders* and *creative thinkers*. These may be united in the same person, often called an *entrepreneur*, or they may exist separately. Certainly every team needs its creative thinkers, whether they are managers or not.

NECESSARY FUNCTIONS

In order to meet the three areas of need, as we have seen, certain functions have to be performed. A function may be defined as the proper or characteristic action of a person or thing. It is often one of a group of related actions, each contributing to a large action. For example, I write with a pen and in writing this sentence, both hand and eyes are fulfilling their normal and characteristic functions to contribute to a single activity. In a the context of the larger activity of leading, such functions as *defining the task* and *planning* are clearly required.

Assemble a group of children in the playground with a task to perform, with or without appointing a leader, and you should be able to observe some of these functions being performed – or not performed, as the case may be.

THE GENERIC ROLE OF LEADER

So far we have agreed only that there are *three overlapping areas of need* present in all working groups, and that in order to meet them certain key *functions* have to be performed. The next step is the idea that these functions hang together in a set: together they form the core of **the generic role of leader**. The discovery of this generic role crowned a quest by thinkers that began long ago in ancient Athens and China, and was pursued intently in recent times.

Expressed in its simplest form, this generic leader's role consists of:

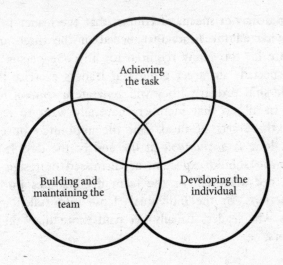

The generic role here is expressed in three very broad functions. It can then be broken down further into more specific functions, such as *planning* and *evaluating*. But you should notice that these functions – and the others explored in Part Two – are not assignable to any one circle: they have effects for good or bad on all three.

For example, 'planning' looks on the surface like a task function. But there is nothing like a bad plan to disintegrate a team, lower morale and frustrate individuals. Planning hits all three circles: the model is a unity, or, more accurately, a diversity-in-unity.

Teams which come together to pursue a self-chosen task, such as trades unions or sports clubs, tend to *elect* their own leaders, who are responsible ultimately to the team. Where tasks are given to the team, on the other hand, the leader tends to be *appointed* by higher authority and sent to it as part of the package deal. In this case the leader is accountable first to the appointing authority and only secondly – if at all – to the team. He or she is responsible for all three circles.

That does not mean, of course, that the leader is going to provide all the functions needed in the three areas – there are far too many required for any one person to do that, especially in larger groups. If leaders exercise the art of leadership properly, they will generate a *sense of responsibility* in all, so that members naturally want to respond to the three sets of need. But the appointed or elected leader alone is *accountable* at the end of the day. It is the leader who should expect to be dismissed or resign if the task is not achieved, or the team disintegrates into warring factions, or the individuals lapse into sullen apathy. That is why leaders usually get paid more than the team members.

Realities of command

Almost everybody thought that it was the French general Marshal Joffre who had won the battle of the Marne in the opening year of the First World War – the crucial battle which had stemmed the advance of the German Army in front of Paris – but some refused to agree. One day a newspaper man appealed to Joffre: 'Will you tell me who did win the battle of the Marne?' 'I can't answer that,' said the Marshal. 'But I can tell you that if the battle of the Marne had been lost the blame would have been on me.'

Understanding your position as the leader in relation to the three circles is vitally important. You should see yourself as half in and half out. There should be some social distance between you and the team, but not too much. The reason for maintaining this element of distance is not to enhance your mystique, it is because you may have to take decisions or act toughly in the task area which will cause reactions to be directed at you from the team and the individuals who face, in consequence, some unwelcome change. You have weakened yourself if you are on too friendly terms, or rather you have exposed yourself to pressures – 'we didn't expect that from *you*' – which you may not be able to handle.

There is an particular problem for leaders who are elected or appointed from among their colleagues and remain with the same team. To exchange the close, friendly relationship of colleagues for those of a leader and subordinates is not easy. That has been recognized for many years. When the Roman Army appointed a man to be a centurion he was always given a century of a hundred men in another legion. The principle is a sound one.

You can begin to see why a degree of self-sufficiency is important for a leader. Leadership is not about popularity, as I have already said, but because leaders tend to have

The lessons of experience

Douglas McGregor was a famous exponent of the 'human relations' school of management in North America, which drew its main inspiration from the Group Dynamics movement. He acted as teacher and consultant to many organizations. In 1948 he was appointed President of Antioch College in America. After about two years he had the honesty to admit that he had made some wrong assumptions about leadership.

'Before coming to Antioch I had observed and worked with top executives as an adviser in a number of organizations. I thought I knew how they felt about their responsibilities and what led them to behave as they did. I even thought that I could create a role for myself that would enable me to avoid some of the difficulties they encountered. I was wrong! It took the direct experience of becoming a line executive, and meeting personally the problems involved, to teach me what no amount of observation of other people could have taught.

I believed, for example, that a leader could operate successfully as a kind of adviser to his organization. I thought I could avoid being a "boss". Unconsciously, I suspect, I hoped to duck the unpleasant necessity of making difficult decisions, or taking the responsibility for one course of action among many uncertain alternatives, of making mistakes and taking the consequences. I thought that maybe I could operate so that everyone would like me – that "good human relations" would eliminate all discord and disagreement.

I could not have been more wrong. It took a couple of years, but I finally began to realize that a leader cannot avoid the exercise of authority any more than he can avoid responsibility for what happens to his organization. In fact, it is a major function of the top executive to take on his own shoulders the responsibility for resolving the uncertainties that are always involved in important decisions. Moreover, since no important decision ever pleases everyone in the organization, he must also absorb the displeasure, and sometimes severe hostility, of those who would have taken a different course.

A colleague recently summed up what my experience has taught me in these words: "A good leader must be tough enough to win a fight, but not tough enough to kick a man when he is down." This notion is not in the least inconsistent with humane, democratic leadership. Good human relations develop out of strength, not weakness.'

W.G. Bennis and E.H. Schein (eds)
Essays of Douglas McGregor (1966)

social, even gregarious, natures, they can find the negative reactions that come their way hard to endure. But what matters in the long run is not how many rounds of applause a leader receives but how much *respect* he or she gains, and that is never achieved by being 'soft' or 'weak' in the task, team or individual circles.

The table on the next page indicates the advantages and disadvantages of a leader's closeness to or distance from the team.

The leader's social needs can be met partly by relations with his or her team, but it is always lonely at the top. He or she can never fully share the burden with those who work for them or open their heart about their own doubts, fears and anxieties; that is best done with other leaders on their own level. If the leader's superior is doing their job they will help to make such meetings possible (they are often called management training courses!). Even more important, the leader's superior should themselves be a resource, a pillar of strength and – at times – a shoulder to weep upon, should the leader require it.

SUMMARY

The third approach to leadership – which in the early days was referred to as 'functional leadership' – concentrated on the third ingredient in any leadership question – the **group** or **team**. The most useful theory about groups for the practical leader is that they are rather like individuals – all unique and yet all having things in common. What they share, according to this theory, is **needs**, just as every individual does. The work of A.H. Maslow forms a useful springboard into the deep water of understanding what makes people 'tick'. These needs are related to **task**, **team maintenance** and the **individual.** These three areas (or circles) *overlap*, for good or ill.

Contrary to the assumptions of some writers in earlier

POSITION OF LEADER IN RELATION TO TEAM		
BEHAVIOUR	**USEFUL**	**NOT USEFUL**
Leader emphasizes distance.	Where team knew him or her well before he became a leader. When team seems to want over-familiarity. When unpopular decisions are in the offing. When taking charge initially of a new team.	Where a team already has a strong traditional sense of distance from its leaders. When people can be fully trusted not to become too familiar anyway.
Leader minimizes distance.	When there is lack of communication and trust between management and employees. Where all are roughly equal in knowledge and experience.	Where the distance is already fairly minimal owing to the predecessor's style. Where it can be misinterpreted as familiarity.
Leader strikes balance between closeness and distance.	Most working situations.	Where the team needs corrective treatment after either too-remote or too-friendly leadership.

days, the roles of leader and members should not be confused. Leaders in real situations are appointed or elected, or they emerge – usually a combination of two of these methods. All good team members will share a sense of responsibility of 'ownership' for the three areas, but it is the appointed or elected leader who is responsible for all three.

By performing – or overseeing the performance of – the *functions of leadership*, as set out more fully in Part Two, the leader guides the group to achieve the task, to maintain its cohesiveness and work as a team, and to enable each individual member to make their optimum contribution. What is now clear is that to be an effective leader in your own field you need the motivation, skills and experience to fulfil the universal or generic role of leader, namely:

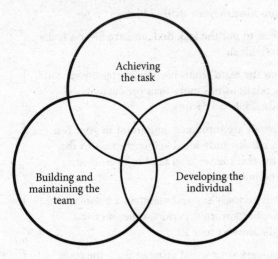

Until you can do this essential work, your appointment as a leader will not be ratified in the hearts and minds of the team.

CHECKLIST:
THE THREE CIRCLES MODEL

	Yes	No
Have you been able to give specific examples from your own experience on how the three circles or areas of need – task, team and individual – interact with each other?	☐	☐

Can you identify your natural bias:

	Yes	No
You tend to put the task first, and are low on team and individual.	☐	
For you the team seems more important; you value happy relationships more than productivity or individual job satisfaction.	☐	
Individuals are supremely important to you; you always put the individual before the task or the team for that matter. You tend to over-identify with the individual.	☐	
You can honestly say you maintain a balance, and have feedback from superiors, colleagues and subordinates to prove it.	☐	
Do you vary your social distance from the team according to a realistic appreciation of the factors in the situation?	☐	☐
Can you illustrate that from experience?	☐	☐

4

PULLING THE THREADS TOGETHER

You can be appointed a manager, but you are not a leader until your appointment is ratified in the hearts and minds of the people.

The discovery of the generic role of leader, as outlined in this book, has proved to be incredibly useful to those who want to improve their capabilities as leaders. In the leadership field it is a breakthrough comparable in a modest way to the discoveries of Newton or Einstein in their field of physics. Like their theoretical advances, the generic role of leadership has proved to be rich in practical applications – the theme of Chapter 5.

LEADERSHIP OR MANAGEMENT

We now have a general theory that integrates both leadership and management in harmony. You may recall that since the day of Frederick W. Taylor and 'Scientific Management', *planning* and *controlling* were the very definition of the work of a manager. Now, thanks to our advance in knowledge, we see them as two functions among many that make up the generic leader role. This is a harmonious whole, with its threads woven together into a pattern.

The early management theorists tended to think of functions, such as planning or controlling, in monochrome terms of one circle only, namely the task. They were one-dimensional. By contrast, the 'functional leadership' approach, which stems from the generic role of leader described in Chapter 3, sees the functions as touching upon all three circles, either directly or indirectly. Moreover, it adds other new functions, especially in the team maintenance area.

It follows that a *good* manager or commander, head or chief, in any field will by definition fulfil the generic role of leader within their specific context of work. So all good leaders, whatever their job titles or fields of employment, will have what I called in Chapter 1 a family resemblance.

SHARING DECISIONS

For many, the word 'leadership' implies that one person is the dictator: he or she makes all the decisions and does all the work of leadership. That is wrong. In groups of more than two or three there are too many functions required for any one person to do it all themselves. The good leader evokes or draws forth leadership from the group. He or she works as a senior partner with other members to achieve the task, build the team and meet individual needs. The ways in which this sharing takes place are so rich and varied that they cannot be prescribed. But a leader who does not capitalize on the natural response of people to the three areas of need hardly deserves the name.

Most practical leaders will accept that other members can help them to maintain the team or motivate and develop fellow individuals. But what about the task? And, in particular, what about *decision making* and *problem solving*? For these are key activities in the task area. It is useful for you as a leader to know the options open to you in decision making or problem solving.

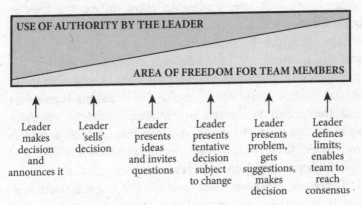

USE OF AUTHORITY BY THE LEADER

AREA OF FREEDOM FOR TEAM MEMBERS

| Leader makes decision and announces it | Leader 'sells' decision | Leader presents ideas and invites questions | Leader presents tentative decision subject to change | Leader presents problem, gets suggestions, makes decision | Leader defines limits; enables team to reach consensus |

Decision making continuum

The model above is simple: it uses the metaphor that a decision is like a cake that can be shared in different ways between the leader and the team as a whole or any individual member. At one end of the continuum the leader has virtually all the cake: he or she issues an order or command. The next point on the line is where the leader says what is to be done but gives reasons; persuades. The remaining four points on the continuum – the different shares of the cake – are fairly self-evident.

You should always bear in mind an important general principle: that the more you move to the right of the continuum the better, for *the more that people share in the decisions which affect their working life the more they are motivated to carry them out.* And as a leader you are in the business of motivator.

But there are factors which you should take into account in deciding where to decide. These include the **situation**, especially such variables as the time available and the complexity or specialized nature of the problem itself.

Thus, the model can help you to develop a satisfactory understanding of why leadership takes different shapes in organizations which work characteristically in *crisis* situations – those in which by definition time is in very short supply and where there is a life-and-death dimension, such as the emergency or military services, civil airlines and operating-theatre teams. Here leaders make the decisions themselves and the group is trained to respond promptly to them without argument. Research at the scenes of road accidents and forest fires confirm that people expect such firm and definite leadership from one person – they need it.

There are other variables, such as the **organization** (values, tradition) and the **group** (knowledge, experience), which you should also take into account in deciding where to decide. You should always aim to be *consistent* as a person so that people know where they stand with you – but when it comes to decision making, infinitely *flexible*.

DEVELOPING YOUR OWN STYLE OF LEADERSHIP

Much argument has raged over 'styles of leadership'. In the early days these styles were labelled by American theorists as 'autocratic', 'democratic' or 'laissez-faire' (or 'do-as-you-please'). That kind of thinking still lingers on.

Decision making and style should not be confused. Style implies much more than decision making. Nor is it possible to alter your 'style', which is an expression of yourself from situation to situation – even if you could – without running the risk of insincerity. You do not want to be a manipulator.

As you may have guessed, I do not find the division into various labelled 'styles' of leadership very helpful. It does not form part of the functional leadership approach.

Indeed I am very wary of thinking too much about one's style as a leader at all. For I believe that style should not be something you arrive at consciously; it should arise naturally or subconsciously as you master the functions or skills of leadership.

'I should like to put on record', wrote the famous author Samuel Butler, 'that I never took the smallest pains with my style, have never thought about it, and do not know or want to know whether it is a style at all or whether it is not, as I believe and hope, just common, simple straightforwardness.' Once your personal style has developed, it will be as difficult to change as your handwriting. It will be your unique way of doing what is common – the truth of leadership, but the truth through the prism of your personality. As a Frenchman in the eighteenth century said, 'These things are external to the man; style is the person.'

DRAWING UPON THE QUALITIES APPROACH

From the new perspective of the generic role, the qualities traditionally associated with leadership (see Chapter 1) can be seen in a new light. They can be interpreted as helping (or hindering) the three areas of need – achieving the task, building or maintaining the team, and developing the individual. First, you should apply the Three Circles model to all the qualities you associate with leadership in order to pick out all the essential ones – those that can be developed. Some qualities will begin to disclose functions and specific behaviours, while some functions and outward actions will imply or express qualities. Some examples are given in the table over the page.

LEADERSHIP CHARACTERISTICS		
	QUALITY	**FUNCTIONAL VALUE**
TASK	*Initiative*	A quality which appears in many research lists. It means the aptitude for initiating or beginning action; the ability to get the group moving.
	Perseverance	The ability to endure; tenacity. Obviously functional in many situations where the group is inclined to give up or is prey to frustrations.
TEAM	*Integrity*	The capacity to integrate; to see the wood for the trees; to bind up parts into a working whole; the attribute that creates a group climate of trust.
	Humour	Invaluable for relieving tension in group or individual, or, for that matter, in the leader themselves. Closely related to a sense of proportion – a useful asset in anything involving people!
INDIVIDUAL	*Tact*	This expresses itself in action by showing sensitive perception of what is fit, or consideration in dealing with others.
	Compassion	Individuals may develop personal problems both at home and work. The leader can show sympathetic awareness of this distress together with a desire to alleviate it.

Some qualities are especially important because they apply to all three circles – *enthusiasm* is an excellent example. Not all enthusiasts are leaders, but if you have the gift of enthusiasm you will almost always spark it off in other people. It produces greater commitment to the task, creates team spirit and enthuses the individual.

Other qualities are more latent. They can be called out

and express themselves in behaviour in any of the three areas. *Moral courage* and *humility*, to give two examples, are both required in certain situations. But it is important to be as specific as possible in defining when they are needed. Humility may seem an odd word because it implies to many people a cringing self-abasement quite at odds with the self-confidence, even egoism, which marks many leaders. Not so when you translate it into terms of task, team and individual.

As Aristotle taught long ago, a virtue rests somewhere between two extremes. If you any quality to excess, or without the moderating influences of balancing qualities, it can become a liability. Certainly too much humility – or rather humility of the counterfeit sort – is fatal to leadership, for it robs you of the proper self-confidence you should have. 'We are all worms,' Winston Churchill once told Lady Violet Bonham-Carter, 'but I do believe I am a glow worm.'

Obviously it would take up too much time and space here to work through all the qualities most frequently mentioned with regard to leadership, seeing them as aptitudes to acquiring or providing certain functional responses – but, taking humility as an example, the table on page 61 explores the degree to which this quality is useful in the three different areas of need.

Humility in action

'A sense of humility is a quality I have observed in every leader whom I have deeply admired,' wrote Eisenhower. 'I have seen Winston Churchill with humble tears of gratitude on his cheeks as he thanked people for their help to Britain and the Allied cause.' He continued: 'My own conviction is that every leader should have enough humility to accept, publicly, the responsibility for the mistakes of the subordinates he has himself selected and, likewise, to give them credit, publicly, for their triumphs. I am aware that some popular theories of leadership hold that the top man must always keep his "image" bright and shining. I believe, however, that in the long run fairness and honesty, and a generous attitude towards subordinates and associates, pay off.'

In a memorial speech on Eisenhower delivered to Congress in 1969, the President of the United States cited as the key to Eisenhower's character an undelivered statement prepared for broadcast over the radio in the event of the D-Day landings ending in disaster. It read as follows.

'Our landings in the Cherbourg-Havre area have failed to gain a satisfactory foothold and I have withdrawn the troops. My decision to attack at this time and place was based upon the best information available. The troops, the airforce and navy, did all that bravery and devotion to duty could do. If any blame or fault attaches to the attempt it is mine alone.'

You can begin to see how the **qualities** and **functions** of leadership fit together like hand in glove. Functions are the active verbs that tell you *what* to do; qualities are the adverbs that inform *how* you do it. As the Chinese say, 'The wings carry the bird; the bird carries the wings.'

THE DIFFERENT LEVELS OF LEADERSHIP

Leadership exists on three broad levels:

Team   Leading a team or small group of about five to fifteen or sixteen people.
Operational Leading a significant part of the business with more than one team leader reporting to you.
Strategic   Leading the whole organization.

HUMILITY IN LEADERSHIP		
AREA	**USEFUL**	**NOT USEFUL**
TASK	When you have clearly made a mistake and you ought to own up to that fact, not blame others.	Apologising for oneself or one's performance all the time.
TEAM	Where the leader is conspicuously lacking in arrogant or assertive behaviour; not abrasive or divisive. Emphasising the group before selfish interest; sharing praise generously.	Showing too much deference or submission to the group.
INDIVIDUAL	Expressing equal value; recognising superior qualities or abilities; giving credit where it is due.	Boot-licking of any kind.

The same generic role – symbolised by the Three Circles model – is present in each level. What differs with level is *complexity*. For example, planning is relatively simple at team level compared with the kind of strategic planning that the chief executive officer of a large organization needs to deliver.

'An institution is the lengthened shadow of one man,' wrote Emerson. It used to be assumed that all that was needed was a great strategic leader. This is not true. What all organizations need is excellence of leadership at *all* levels – team, operational and strategic – and good teamwork between the levels of responsibility.

LEADERSHIP AND VALUES

'Is there not a difference', John Lord (the Academy Sergeant
Major at Sandhurst during my time there) asked me once,
'between *good leaders* and *leaders for good*?'

The original Three Circles model spoke only about needs.
But it is impossible to keep values out of the picture, even if
anyone wanted to do so. You have values as well as needs and
they play a vital part in your decisions. Actually the relationship between values and needs is very close – we need
what we value; we value what we need. But they are different.
Good and bad, truth and falsehood, right and wrong, are not
needs but they do affect conduct.

You may think this is a philosophical point, not a practical
one. But the best leaders have something of the philosopher
in them. The fact that we are valuing humans as well as
needing humans has implications which are best understood
with reference again to the Three Circles model. Viewed
through the microscope of values we should have to search
out answers to the following questions.

Task   Why is this task worthwhile? What is its value
to society? How is that value measured?

Team   What is the commonly accepted framework of
values – including ethics – that holds this team
together?

Individual   Do I hold the same values as this team? Is the
task worthwhile in my eyes?

Some people can do this kind of valuing arithmetic quite
easily for themselves. But you as the leader will have to show
awareness of the values of the common enterprise and
interpret them for people both inside the team and outside

it. Task, team and individual have to be related in values as well as in needs. That is why true leadership has an inescapable moral, or even spiritual, dimension. Without it some people may call you a *good leader* in the technical sense of the word – but you will not be a *leader for good.*

SUMMARY

The Three Circles model in its active form serves as a catalyst. It blends together invisibly the three main approaches to understanding leadership – qualities, situational and group or functional – into one integrated whole.

*A leader is the kind of person (**qualities**), with the appropriate knowledge (**situational**), who is able to provide the necessary skills (**functions**) to enable a group to achieve its task, to hold it together as a cohesive team and to motivate and develop individuals – and he or she does so in partnership with the right level of participation of other members of the group or organization.*

Now this cumbersome sentence is clearly not meant to stand alone as a definition. But it is a way in which I can pull together the threads for you.

By necessity leadership itself has to be something of a team effort, especially as you move into the higher levels of leadership. Or, to put it another way, your team becomes one which is composed of leaders within the organization. Sometimes I think that *all* members of an organization today should be viewed as leaders. You need to fulfil – to master – the generic role. Your style, which is an expression of you, will then emerge naturally as you apply yourself to the simple functions of leadership. For leadership does consist mainly in doing some relatively simple and straightforward things, and doing them extremely well.

At whatever level of leadership you find yourself, you should think and communicate about the task in terms of values as well as needs. Then the common purpose will tend to be in harmony with the values of your team and all the individuals in the organization – including your own.

5

SOME PRACTICAL APPLICATIONS

**'There is nobody who cannot improve
their powers of leadership by a little
thought and practice.'**
Field Marshal Lord Slim

The earliest practical application of the broad ideas in this book was to the leadership selection field. Before 1942 the British Army relied exclusively on the interview method. A selection committee interviewed the candidate for a commission and tried to identify those with the essential qualities. As you can imagine, this was something of a hit-or-miss affair.

When Field Marshal Lord Montgomery was an officer cadet at Sandhurst his Company Commander called him into his office for an interview.

'Montgomery,' he said, 'I have been watching you very carefully and I have to tell you that you will never be promoted above the rank of major.'

'Well,' said the Field Marshal in a talk on leadership to the Sandhurst officer cadets which I had the good fortune to hear. 'Well, he was wrong. It was *he* who never rose above the rank of major!'

LEADERSHIP SELECTION

In order to cope with the numbers and improve effectiveness (large numbers – up to 50 per cent – selected by the interview method were being returned to their units from the officer training schools as unfit to be leaders), a team of psychologists and officers devised the three-day War Officer Selection Board. Many decades later it is still in use by Britain's armed services because it was constructed on such sound principles.

At the centre of the selection process lay a number of practical exercises. The candidate was put in charge of a small group with a simple task to perform against the clock. The psychologists were aware of the early work in America on 'the dynamics of interpersonal relations'. They had also grasped the significance of the situational approach – not bad for 1942.

In particular they knew that they were looking for leaders who could operate under the stress conditions of battle. While the candidate was leading the group the observers looked at and evaluated (in the words of one of them) the following behaviours.

1. The effective **level of his functioning**: his ability to contribute towards the functional aspect of the common task by planning and organizing the available resources such as abilities, materials and time.
2. His **group cohesiveness** or ability to bind the group in the direction of the common task: to relate its members emotionally to each other and to the task.
3. His **stability** (or **mental stamina**): the ability to stand up to resistance and frustrations without serious impairment of 1 or 2 and the results of their interplay.

In other words, the candidate was tested *in* a group *for* a group. Interviews, intelligence and aptitude testings, the giving of short talks and short role plays supplemented this core of exercises.

The full history of the War Office Selection Boards has yet to be written, but it is generally accepted that the WOSB introduced by the British Army in 1942 is the ancestor of all our management or leadership assessment centres today. It was a remarkable social innovation.

TRAINING FOR LEADERSHIP

It was one thing to *select* leaders using the WOSB method but it was quite another thing to *train* leaders. Although some early attempts during the Second World War to train for leadership were made, the general climate – as we have seen – was against it. You were either a born leader or you were not.

'Smith is not a born leader yet,' wrote one Sandhurst company commanding officer about one of his officer cadets, as we saw in Chapter 1. But what could Smith do about it? What, for that matter, could Sandhurst do about it? Leadership instruction at Sandhurst in 1960 consisted of lectures of the qualities of leadership as listed by Slim and other British generals. Officer cadets, weary from their military training, tended to fall asleep in their comfortable chairs during these periods.

Paradoxically, it was two undoubted 'born leaders' who first challenged the old assumption. Field Marshal Lord Slim's ringing words stand at the head of this chapter. Montgomery, the other great British 'born leader', was equally convinced that leadership could be developed.

Well, can leaders be trained?

Some will say that leaders are born, not made, and that you can't make a leader by teaching, or training. I don't agree with this entirely. While it is true that some men have within themselves the instincts and qualities of leadership in a much greater degree than others, and some men will never have the character to make leaders, I believe that leadership can be developed by training. In the military sphere, I reckon that soldiers will be more likely to follow a leader in whose military knowledge they have confidence, rather than a man with much greater personality but with not the same obvious knowledge of his job. To the junior leader himself the mere fact of responsibility brings courage; the mere fact that by his position as the recognized head of a group of men he is responsible for their lives and comfort, gives him less time to think of his own fears and so brings him a greater degree of resolution than if he were not the leader. I know I found this to be the case myself in 1914, when as a young lieutenant I commanded a platoon and had to lead them in charges against entrenched Germans, or undertake patrol activities in no-man's land. By the training I had received from my superiors in peacetime, I gained confidence in my ability to deal with any situation likely to confront a young officer of my rank in war; this increased my morale and my powers of leading my platoon, and later my company.

In other words, it is almost true to say that leaders are 'made' rather than born. Many men who are not natural leaders may have some small spark of the qualities which are needed; this spark must be looked for, and then developed and brought on by training. But except in the armed forces this training is not given. In civilian circles it seems to be considered that leadership descends on men 'like dew from heaven' – it does not. There are principles of leadership just as there are principles of war, and these have to be studied.

Field Marshal Viscount Montgomery

Both Slim and Montgomery lectured and wrote on the theme of leadership in the years after the Second World War, and they did so in a way that encouraged others to believe that they could grow as leaders. Not surprisingly, they framed their thoughts in the language of leadership qualities, for they had grown up in a world where the only language about leadership was the language of qualities.

As a civilian lecturer in military history I worked at the Royal Military Academy, Sandhurst, from 1961 to 1969. It was my work there that expanded the vocabulary of leadership and opened the door to the new era. At Sandhurst I had the opportunity of evolving, together with a committee of officers, a functional leadership course based upon the Three Circles model. We ran the first experimental course in 1962 and Sandhurst as a whole adopted the approach two years later to supplement its traditional teaching on leadership qualities. Thereafter, as Adviser on Leadership Training, I was responsible both for the quality of the two-day course, which was run by company commanders, and also for relating it to practical leadership training in the field. It soon proved that the basic principles in this book could be successfully applied to developing leaders in the civilian field as well as in the military.

What was new about this course, apart from its group-centred learning methods, was the introduction of theory. As I explained in the Introduction to this book, it is when sparks jump both ways between theory and practice that learning occurs.

The programme was designed not to *teach* leadership but to give young officers-to-be the opportunity to *learn* about it, to make discoveries as they explored their own experience in the light of the principles of leadership.

Functional leadership as a form of training had certain hallmarks from the beginning.

Simple	'Simple, but not superficial or simplistic' – as little jargon as possible.
Practical	Concerned with practical, how-to-do-it functions and actions of leadership, not abstract or academic theory for its own sake.
Participative	Exercises, case studies and checklists to involve you in the process of learning. That makes it enjoyable as well as useful.

In the 1990s The Industrial Society in London with my help made functional leadership much more widely available. In that process it was renamed Action Centred Leadership. It did, however, retain the essential characteristics of simple, practical and participative.

Leader's checklist

1. Set the task of the team; put it across with enthusiasm and remind people of it often.
2. Instruct all leaders in the three circles; make them accountable for teams of four to fifteen.
3. Plan the work, pace its progress and design jobs to encourage the commitment of individuals and teams.
4. Set individual gargets after consulting; discuss progress with each person regularly but at least once a year.
5. Delegate decisions to individuals. Consult those affected.
6. Communicate the importance of each person's job; explain decisions to help people apply them; brief team monthly on Progress, Policy and People.
7. Train and develop people, especially those under twenty-five; gain support for the rules and procedures, set an example and 'have a go' at those who break them.
8. Where unions are recognized, encourage joining, attendance at meetings, standing for office and speaking up for

what each person believes is in the interest of the task, team and individual.

9. Care about the wellbeing of people in the team; improve working conditions; deal with grievances and attend functions.

10. Monitor action; learn from successes and mistakes; regularly walk round each person's place of work; observe, listen and praise.

The Industrial Society

In my first book in this field, *Training for Leadership* (1968), I tell the story of the introduction and evolution of Functional Leadership at Sandhurst, and its adoption by the Royal Air Force and the Royal Navy. The book also described some early applications in industry and commerce which indicated that training for leadership was as effective with managers as it had been with commanders-to-be.

One of the first people to write to me after the publication of *Training for Leadership* – in his characteristically clear handwriting – was Field Marshal Lord Montgomery, now firmly persuaded that leadership could be taught in the way I had described. He added: 'Leadership is an immense subject. Nowhere is it more important to teach it than at Sandhurst and in our universities; in fact to youth, since it falls on dead ground with the older generation.'

Ten years later, after becoming what proved to be the world's first Professor of Leadership Studies, I have been able to introduce leadership training courses based on the principles in this book to engineering students at the University of Surrey. The courses have continued to this day. There is ample evidence that young people destined to work in industry, commerce or the public service are eager to explore the nature of good leadership and have some practical training for it. For there is a widespread sense that 'what the world needs now is not bosses but leaders'.

THE TEST OF EXPERIENCE

'Time tests truth,' according to an English proverb. Einstein said much the same: whereas it is experiment that establishes truth in science, it is experience that performs the same function in human affairs.

The philosopher Karl Popper advanced the important principle that in science it is impossible to prove that a hypothesis or theory is actually true: what can be done – by persistent experimentation – is to falsify it if it is falsifiable. It is that which withstands such repeated and varied attempts to falsify it that accumulates even stronger grounds for being accepted as – to all intents and purposes – true.

It follows that the process of testing a theory in the non-science context is bound to be a lengthy one. Consequently it has taken over fifty years before the truth of the Three Circles model has begun to be evident.

THE STORY OF ICI

'Can you point us to an organization that is growing leaders?' they asked me. Silence fell in my room, and I gazed out of the window, reflecting.

At the time I was the first Professor of Leadership Studies, and so my two visitors to the university understandably expected me to know the answer. 'Not the armed forces,' they added, 'we have already been to see them.'

Well, I could think of plenty of companies that were *training* leaders – sending their first-line managers, for example, on action-centred leadership courses – but that was not the question they asked. Who is *growing* leaders?

'I cannot think of anyone,' I replied eventually.

'All right then,' they said, 'We will do it. Will you help us?'

I agreed to do so, and they told me more about their situation. My visitors, Bill Stead and Edgar Vincent, were the senior group human resources managers in ICI, then known as 'the bellwether of British industry'. (A 'bellwether' is literally the leading sheep of a flock, the practice being to hang a bell around its neck.)

Their particular bell was already tinkling the death knell of old-style management in the UK. Not that the rest of the flock had ears to hear it. In 1988, Bill and Edgar told me, the profits of ICI fell by a staggering 48 per cent; the dividend was cut for the first time since the formation of the company in 1926. ICI was too large (over 60,000 employees), too bureaucratic and in the wrong markets. The main board executive directors had decided that ICI's top priority was to develop 'manager-leaders' – the first time, I recall, that I had ever heard that particular phrase.

Over the next five years we went about 'growing leaders' in the nine divisions of ICI. *After five years ICI was the first British company in history to make a billion pounds' profit.*

The bedrock of the transformation of ICI during those astonishing four or five years was the application of the Three Circles model and my practical philosophy to all levels of management in the nine divisions. A critical mass of ICI's managers and supervisors moved from being mere managers to becoming 'manager-leaders'.

Sir John Harvey-Jones, the Chairman of ICI during this period, proved to be an outstanding strategic leader and it was a pleasure to work with him. He was generous in giving credit to the contribution of my functional leadership approach, writing that 'John Adair is without doubt one of the foremost thinkers on leadership in the world'. And in 2007 he kindly presented me with the first Lifetime Award in the field of leadership development.

SUMMARY

The concept of the Three Circles model and the functional leadership approach has been widely applied and thoroughly tested. Indeed, no other leadership theory in the world has survived so long. In this chapter I have described two major applications – to selection and to training – in the armed services, and one to developing leadership in a large industrial organization.

This brief review should, I hope, give you the confidence to take the generic role of leader as the basis for your own self-development as a leader.

If you do look upon this book as your personal action-centred leadership course, you should work through the rest of it with pen and paper at hand ready to write down any *action points* which occur to you. This should be done immediately after the end of *each* chapter – don't wait until the end of the book. The action points should be as specific as possible, focusing on such areas as:

- Your performance as a leader
- Your own learning and training needs
- Points for your working group
- Possible changes in the organization
- Longer-term self-development goals.

PART TWO

DEVELOPING YOUR LEADERSHIP ABILITIES

The next eight chapters focus on the main practical **functions** that you will certainly have to perform or manage as a leader. They are deliberately not grouped under task, team and individual, for you should constantly remember that the circles overlap: therefore any function will affect all three.

For instance, **planning** may seem to be a task function initially, but there is nothing like a bad plan to break up group unity or frustrate the individual. The functions are like the white and black keys on a piano: they will have to be played in different sequences and combined in chords if you want to make music.

By the time you have finished reading and working upon Part Two you should:

• Be able to identify clearly the main **functions** or **principles** of leadership in the three areas and have a good idea of how they manifest themselves in practice.

- Know what constitutes **skill** in providing those functions in certain kinds of situation.
- Be able to establish the **abilities** that you need to develop in yourself if you are going to be successful in providing those functions over a long and varied career.

6

DEFINING THE TASK

*'Keep the general goal in sight while
tackling daily tasks.'*
Chinese proverb

Your primary responsibility as a leader is to ensure that your group achieves its common task. Leadership is sometimes defined as 'getting other people to do what *you* want to do because *they* want to do it'. I do not agree. If it is *your* task, why should anyone help you to achieve it? It has to be a *common* task, one which everyone in the group can share because they see that it has value for the organization or society and – directly or indirectly – for themselves as well.

Remember that achieving the task is your principal means of developing high morale and meeting individual needs. What you do (or fail to do) in the task area is bound to affect the other two circles, the team and the individual. So you should bear those two spheres in mind when you commit yourself and the group to task action.

As the leader you cannot perform all the functions yourself. The group is not a flock of sheep – passive, walking lumps of mutton – with yourself as the human shepherd. They can help you and you can help them in pursuit of the common goal in various ways. The group members have energy, enthusiasm, experience, knowledge, ability or skill, and often creative ideas, to contribute to the key task functions.

The actual technologies involved in the task will obviously vary from group to group. But it is possible to pick out some general functions that have to be fulfilled in any working group if it is to be successful. Inevitably, without the 'clothes' of a particular business upon them these functions will look rather naked, but they are the essential raw materials of leadership.

COMMUNICATING THE OBJECTIVE

Your first aim as a leader is to make the task truly common by communicating or sharing it – that is, assuming that you have been given a definite objective by your superior which the group does not know about. But that is only one type of situation, a relatively straightforward one. You may be in a group that is responsible for defining its own objectives under your leadership, or the responsibility for defining objectives may rest upon your shoulders. But, firstly, what exactly is an *objective*?

You may have noted already that 'task' is a fairly general word. It means a work required by an employer or a situation. Tasks come in different shapes and sizes. They are also often gift-wrapped in misleading terms. The leader, either on his or her own or with others, may have to bend their analytical powers of mind to penetrate the core of the task. One vital question is, 'How will we know when we have succeeded?' If that question cannot be answered it is usually a sign that the task is not yet clear enough.

You can visualize tasks in terms of different sizes. Personally I find it useful to distinguish between **purpose**, **aims** and

objectives. Others prefer to make a rough distinction between 'short-term' and 'long-term' objectives. The dictionary will not help you here: the English language uses such words rather loosely. It is obvious, however, that there is a difference between the broader, less defined 'aim' and the more tangible or definite 'objective'.

I shall define the terms 'objective', 'aim' and 'purpose' below but, firstly, the following example may help to illustrate the differences between these types of task. It shows what is involved in – and what to avoid – in communicating the objective.

> Windlesham Ltd are in the business of making bath plugs. You could call that their *purpose*. They have two *aims*: to make the best bath plugs in the world and to capture 60 per cent of the world market in the next three years (they have 35 per cent at present). Jane Jackson is just one team leader at their Chobham factory. The *objective* this week for her section is to make 30,000 one-inch plugs for a new town in Saudi Arabia.

Defining the task is not something you have to do only at the beginning of an enterprise – confusion about the end of a task can soon invade a group or organization. So you should be ready to define the end that the team or any given individual is presently working towards whenever the need arises.

PURPOSE, AIMS AND OBJECTIVES

I mentioned above the distinction I favour between purpose, aims and objectives. My definitions of these terms are as follows.

Purpose   The overarching, general or integrating task of the group or organization.

Your defined purpose answers the *why* questions – 'Why are we in business?' 'Why are we doing this?' It can signify, too, the content of value or meaning in what you are doing.

Human nature craves meaning, and so if your purpose connects with personal and moral values you will not find it difficult to generate a *sense of purpose* in your team – and here *purpose* means *energy*. Your team organization will be under way, like a ship at sea.

Purpose is not the same as *vision*. A vision is a mental picture of what you want the team or the organization to look like or be in, say, three years' time.

Aims   You can break purpose down into *aims*, which are open-ended but directional. 'To become a better violinist' is an aim. You can have several – 'to improve my skills as a cook', for another example. But you shouldn't have too many, for your time and resources are limited. And that is also true of teams and organizations. So once you have identified purpose, choose aims carefully.

Objectives   *Objectives* are far more tangible, definite, concrete and time-bounded. The word comes from a shortening of the military phrase 'objective point'.

A familiar picture-word or metaphor for objective is *target*, originally the mark at which archers shot their arrows. A target is tangible and visible. You can clearly see the arrows sticking in the outer and inner rings or the bullseye.

A *goal* is another such picture-word. A football match takes place within clearly defined limits of space and time; players can see instantly if they score a goal. If they are frustrated they can go and kick the goalposts! To score goals in a match or to reach the finishing line in a marathon race calls for prolonged effort and hardship, and those overtones often colour the use of the word 'goal' in ordinary working life.

Always remember that an **objective** should be tangible, concrete, limited in time; an **aim** is less defined but is still fairly substantial rather than abstract; but a **purpose** may be couched in general or value terms.

THE REASON WHY

The apparently quite simple behaviour of a leader telling a group what to do in fact discloses several distinct levels of mental ability. These cannot be directly associated with the levels of leadership, incidentally, although there ought to be some co-relation between them. These can be identified for you, along with some common mistakes to avoid (see table over the page, 'Communicating the objective').

Perhaps the key ability for you to focus on first is the ability to break down the *general* into the *particular*. Aristotle taught his pupil, the future Alexander the Great, the simple lesson of how to take a general intention and turn it into a

COMMUNICATING THE OBJECTIVE	
ABILITIES	**MISTAKES TO AVOID**
Telling the group the objective you have been given.	Not understanding it yourself first. Indistinctness or lack of clarity in briefing ('I thought you said two-inch plugs, Jane'). So check understanding.
Telling the group not only *what* to do, but also *why*.	Giving the reason in terms of a past event rather than the future. ('Why are we doing it, Jane?' 'That's simple. The boss told me to do it'. A better answer would be: 'That Saudi Arabian order is vital if we are going to achieve our marked share aim in the Middle East'.)
Breaking down an aim into objectives for other groups.	Not making the objectives specific enough. Leaving parts of the aim uncovered by objectives, so that the objectives do not together add up to fulfilling the aim.
Agreeing the objective.	Taking things for granted. ('Sorry we didn't complete your Saudi Arabian order, Peter. I had three other rush orders on and two machines out of action. I could have told you we couldn't do it'.)
Relating aim to purpose so that you can answer the questions 'Why are we doing it?'; 'In order to achieve what?'.	Confusing our department's aim with the organization's purpose. ('Henry, we are solely in business to make the world's best plugs.' 'Nonsense, Peter, only one things matters: what we are really after is to get as big a market share as possible and to make as much money as we can.')

Defining purpose and checking that aims relate to it and to each other.	Not doing it often enough. ('Come on, Peter and Henry, Windlesham is in business to produce certain goods at a profit – a high-quality product and a fair market share are both vital to the end. You are team members – not rivals!')
Re-defining purpose; making it more general so as to create more aims and objectives.	Doing it too often. Not sensing that it has to be done. ('Since I became managing director of Windlesham's a year ago it has dawned on me that we are really in the business of equipping bathrooms. Why not make the baths for our plugs?')
Communicating purpose to the shop floor.	Using the wrong language. Completely by-passing leaders below you. Relying solely on others to do it for you.

specific objective. (That is why Alexander was able to conquer the known world! Unfortunately he eventually ran out of both world and time, but that is another story.) All leaders need this skill of quarrying objectives out of aims, and then cutting *steps* into the objectives so that the objectives can be achieved. Or, as a proverb puts it more colourfully, 'If you are going to eat an elephant you have to do it one mouthful at a time.'

The reverse process – relating the *particular* to the *general* – is equally important. Leaders tend naturally to give *the reason why* something has to be done; bosses just tell you to do it. Answering the question 'why' means connecting it in the group's mind with the larger ongoing aims or purposes.

SUMMARY

Within the compass of the three circles, **defining the task** is a vital leadership function. 'Task' is a general word. It needs to be broken down into **purpose**, **aims** and **objectives**.

Aims arise when *purpose* is directed and harnessed. As a leader you should be able to range up and down from the particular to the general within the task circle. Such thinking is the necessary preliminary to *communication*.

Leadership implies communicating the *why* as well as the *what* and *how*, *when* and *where* and *who* of work that has to be done. A good leader is a forward thinker. He or she answers the question *why*, not with a backward-looking sentence – 'because we have always done it this way' – but with a forward-looking one – 'in order to achieve this aim or that purpose'. Clarity about the task is often difficult to achieve. But it is essential to acquire it yourself and then to share it with others.

> *When people are of one mind and heart they can have Mount Tai.*
>
> Chinese proverb
>
> (Mount Tai is a famous mountain in Shangdon Province – the highest known to Confucius.)

CHECKLIST:
DEFINING THE TASK

	Yes	No
1. Are you clear about the **objectives** of your team now and for the next few years/months, and have you agreed them with your leader?	☐	☐
2. Do you fully understand the wider **aims** and **purpose** of the organization?	☐	☐
3. Can you relate the objectives of your team to those larger, more general intentions?	☐	☐
4. Does your present team objective have sufficient specificity? Is it defined in terms of time? Is it as concrete or tangible as you can make it?	☐	☐
5. Will the team be able to know soon for itself if you succeed or fail? Does it have swift feedback of results?	☐	☐

PLANNING

**'Nothing is particularly hard if you divide
it into small jobs.'**
Henry Ford

Planning is the activity of bridging the gap mentally from
where you and the group are now to where you want to be
at some future moment in terms of accomplishing a task. A
plan is a method devised for making or doing something or
achieving an end. It always implies mental formulation and
sometimes graphic representation.

The planning function is the response to the group's need:
'How are we going to achieve the task?' But the 'how' question
soon leads you to ask also 'Who does what?' and 'When does
it have to be done?' Indeed, as a planner you could do worse
than memorise Rudyard Kipling's short checklist:

> I keep six honest serving men
> (They taught me all I knew);
> Their names are *What* and *Why* and *When*,
> And *How* and *Where* and *Who*.

Usually, if a plan proves to be inadequate it is because either
you as the leader, or the group (or both), have not pressed

home these questions until you have clear and definite answers. A poor or inadequate plan means that your subsequent team action is doomed from the start. It usually turns into a drama, a comedy or tragedy, depending on the circumstances, in three Acts: Beginning, Muddle and No End. As the old adage says, 'Fail to plan and you plan to fail.'

> Calmex, a major paint company, produced a new paint stripper that was three times faster and more effective than the other brands on the market. Helen Robinson, the marketing and public relations director, drew up an advertising plan to support the launch. But one agency failed to produce an important TV commercial on time. When Robinson remonstrated, the agency head got out the plan. 'It says here that you wanted it "as soon as possible". We thought next month would do.'

So planning is essentially about devising a method for making or doing something or achieving an end. A leader without plans is not likely to be effective. So, how do you develop skill as a planner?

SEARCHING FOR ALTERNATIVES

There is a skill in conjuring out from your own mind and from the group a sufficient number of alternative methods to choose from.

Shortage of time obviously can limit you. If you are trying to avoid a car crash you do not have time to consider all the feasible alternatives: you have to select the first one that flashes into your mind. Therefore one of the first questions you should ask is, 'How much time have I got?'

If necessary, test those time constraints to see if they are *real* as opposed to *assumed* ones. We often have more time to make a plan than we think we do. Provided there is not a crisis or an emergency and you know how much time is available, you can apply yourself to using that planning time to good effect. Keep a careful check on the time, however, because it soon goes.

Another factor you must take into account is the resources available to you in identifying the different feasible courses of action or solutions. What *people* can you consult? You may have noticed how good leaders lead when faced with a significant difficulty – whether an operational challenge or some crisis. They hold in check their own hunches or intuitions as to what should be done. Establishing the facts is their absolute priority, coupled with identifying the salient factors, the ones relevant to the decision that needs to be made. Then, when discussing the options that arise from the realities of the situation, the leader tends not to declare his or her own thoughts prematurely. A trained instinct causes the effective leader always to listen first to the ideas, courses of action or solutions proposed by the team. If time allows, he or she asks those junior to speak before their seniors. The leader then summarizes what has been put forward, decides on the way forward, and explains the logic behind it. Such an approach can be deeply satisfying to all participants and is likely to yield the best solution.

The table opposite summarizes the different levels of group participation in decision making, showing under what circumstances these are useful or appropriate.

The team or individuals who are going to carry out the plan are especially important in the decision making process. Remember that fundamental principle: *the more that people share in the decisions which affect their working life the more they are motivated to carry them out.* (See 'Sharing decisions',

Chapter 4.) Think out the appropriate strategy for involving them on the lines of an appreciation of the three degrees of participation described in the table below.

SHARING DECISIONS		
DEGREE OF PARTICIPATION	**USEFUL**	**NOT USEFUL**
1. You present a tentative plan subject to change if another in the group comes up with a better one.	When group time is short. Where you have much experience in the field and are fairly sure you are right.	Where time is plentiful and the group is as technically competent as you are. When you are only going through the motions, being unwilling to accept any changes.
2. You present the problem and get suggestions from the group	It involves the group much more than does option 1. Groups can be far more creative than their individual members – including you. ('Two heads are better than one.')	Can be time-consuming. If the group lacks sufficient knowledge and interest in the matter in hand.
3. You present a firm plan, subject to only minor changes of detail to improve it.	When you are absolutely sure that you are right. Where time is critically short.	Where the group needs to be more involved in the thinking and deciding if it is to be really committed to action.

In the positions shown in the table on the previous page, 'Sharing decisions', (which you may take up in different situations during a single working day) it is assumed that you as the leader will take the decision to do it *this* way rather than *that* way at the end of the first phase of planning. Should you ever allow the group as a whole to take the decision? That depends upon what might be called the 'political constitution' – written or unwritten – of the group or organization, which usually makes these things fairly clear. Some main types of situation can be identified, as shown in the table below.

POSITION OF LEADER IN RELATION TO GROUP	
POSITION	NOTES
You are an **elected** leader, leading the group that elected you.	The group as a whole may well wish to choose between alternative outline plans itself. It may expect you to put the matter to a vote or to test for consensus.
You are an **emergent** leader, without any formal authority at all. The group looks to you for a lead.	You can influence the group to adopt one course rather than another. But, if you want to stay leader, you'll have to go along with the group choice if it contradicts your own judgement. The political constitution will be informal and often vague. Both you and the group may appeal to precedents in decision making.
You are an **appointed** leader, with a clearly defined authority	If you are ultimately accountable for the work of the group, you can justly claim to have the last word on the decision.

As you will see, there are some 'grey areas' in sharing decision making with a group. You may be two, if not all three, of these types of leader. The political leader in many democratic countries where there is a constitutional monarchy or equivalent presidency, for example, is emergent, elected and appointed. Even if you have the authority to propose your own plan and carry it out, or arbitrarily to choose among the several possibilities put forward the one that you personally like best, you may be reluctant to use that authority, for you want to involve and commit the group. But keep a firm control of the process.

In groups where all members are roughly equal in competence the choice between alternatives may be debated hotly. Leaders as well as members need to be able to put the case for a course of action as persuasively as they can, while remaining open-minded and honest enough to recognize the truth when it emerges from any quarter. Such a process is the essence of democracy. 'Whenever people can be persuaded rather than ordered – when they can be made to feel that they have participated in developing the plan – they approach their tasks with understanding and enthusiasm,' said Eisenhower. He recalled that Churchill was a persuader during the planning phase:

> Indeed his skill in the use of words and logic was so great that on several occasions when he and I disagreed on some important matter – even when I was convinced of the correctness of my own view and when responsibility was clearly mine – I had a very hard time withstanding his arguments. More than once he forced me to re-examine my own premises, to convince myself again that I was right – or accept his solution. Yet if the decision went against him, he accepted it with good grace, and did everything in his power to support it with proper action. Leadership by

persuasion and the wholehearted acceptance of a contrary
decision are both fundamentals of democracy.

It becomes clear that without leadership any form of democracy can be inert and feeble.

As the Chinese saying goes, 'A thousand workers, a thousand plans.' To get anything agreed and done calls for
leadership. When all people can feel themselves to be equal
in value, if not in knowledge and experience, that is the
beginning of true leadership – not its end. As Montesquieu
wrote, 'To suggest where you cannot compel, to guide where
you cannot demand, that is the supreme form of skill.'

HOW TO BE MORE CREATIVE

Planning doesn't sound very creative, does it? All those typed
schedules and drawings or diagrams. But a plan grows from
an idea. That idea is the germ of a method, solution or
course. Perhaps the most common mistake is to make an
unconscious assumption which limits the number or kind of
methods. 'It is quite clear', a director of human resources
announced to her colleagues recently, 'that we can do only
two things about Bill Jackson in accounts: move him side-
ways or make him redundant. Which will it be?'

The better leaders have always resisted this binary thinking
– black or white; this or that. But many managers (and
academics) do think in terms of either/or, because it offers a
spurious clarity. This is an important stage in some cases
(e.g. a judge summing up for a jury), to reduce the judgment
to an issue (either this or that) if it can be done. But it is
fatal to do it too quickly, so that you totally ignore the third,
fourth or fifth possibilities, which might have included the
best suggestions. So you should make sure that you or your

group generate enough options. As Bismarck used to say to his generals, 'If you think the enemy has only two courses open to him you can be sure that he will choose the third!'

Alfred P. Sloan, the great President of General Motors in the United States, is reported to have said at a meeting of one of his top committees. 'Gentlemen, I take it we are all in complete agreement on the decision here.' Everyone around the table nodded assent. 'Then', continued Sloan, 'I propose we postpone further discussion of this matter until our next meeting to give ourselves time to develop disagreement and perhaps gain some understanding of what the decision is all about.'

In most situations, the three or four feasible alternatives can be identified by straightforward observation, thought and group discussion. But there is often a 'creative solution', so called because it is hidden until someone actually discovers it. ('How obvious and simple. Why didn't we think of that?') If the two puzzles in the following exercise are not already familiar to you they will make the point.

EXERCISE 5: Creative solutions
1. Connect up the nine dots with four consecutive straight lines, i.e. without taking your pencil off the paper.

2. Take six matchsticks and put them on a table in front of you. Now arrange them into a pattern of four

equilateral (equal-sided) triangles, without breaking the matches. There are at least two acceptable solutions.

Now turn to page 221 for the answers.

Karl Dunckner, the psychologist who invented the above matchsticks problem in the 1920s, made the point that we develop *functional fixedness* as we grow older. So, for example, we view a hammer as only for knocking in nails. The first step towards greater creativity is to try to free ourselves from such assumptions, useful though they are in everyday life.

EXERCISE 6: Functional flexibility
List twenty-five uses for a hammer other than knocking in nails or wrenching them out. You have five minutes.

You may find it hard to think of new ideas or to generate them from other people if you have picked up the habit of instant criticism.

Negative criticism directed at your own ideas or someone else's will destroy them. The technique known as 'brainstorming' works by encouraging people deliberately to *suspend judgement* – to refrain from criticism and to produce as many ideas as possible. On the other hand, if you want to stifle creative thinking here are some useful phrases for you:

'That will never work.'

'Don't waste my time with such rubbish.'

'We have tried it before.'

'If you thought it up it must be wrong.'

The concept of group climate is important here. Some groups are like a white frost on an April morning in England: they kill off the blossoms of ideas which might one day fruit into plans. The atmosphere is negative, hypercritical and anxious. Other groups are like warm mornings in May: positive, encouraging and confident. Leadership is a key factor in turning a negative group into a positive one. One important skill is asking leading questions, as shown in the table on page 96, 'Some skills in generating ideas'.

Each of us has some ten thousand million brain cells and they are probably the most expensive resource your organization hires. In order to secure the best-quality plan you will need to involve the team's brain cells as well as your own. It pays off a high dividend in commitment.

Quality Circles originated in Japan, and from twenty Circles in 1961 a staggering 10 million workers were members of Circles by 1980. Little wonder then that Japan had seized world leadership in quality by the end of the 1980s, especially in the production of motor vehicles and electrical goods. Who would then have thought in 1945 that one day Toyota and Honda would challenge Ford and General Motors for dominance in their own home American market? The general principle behind Quality Circles is simple. A team meets for about one hour every week in company time to discuss work problems, investigate their causes and recommend solutions. These solutions are then implemented directly or presented to management for agreement on action.

MAKING A CONTINGENCY PLAN

Constructing a work programme and a time plan follows naturally from the choice of a method to achieve the task. Depending on the technology involved, that work programme can vary enormously in size and complexity. The

SOME SKILLS IN GENERATING IDEAS	
QUESTIONS/STATEMENTS	NOTES
Bringing in 'Bob, you have had experience in several other industries, how did they tackle this problem?'	Meets individual needs as well as the task.
Stimulating 'Imagine we were starting from scratch again. How would we do it?'	Brains are like car engines. They need warming up by outrageous ideas or thought-provoking suggestions.
Building on 'Can't we develop the idea behind Mary's suggestion of cutting down the number of files? Could we use the computer more? How else can we improve our information storage system?'	Entails seeing the positive idea or principle in a suggestion and taking it further.
Spreading 'We can also include Jim's suggestion about time-keeping and Mary's point about safety in the plan.'	Helps to develop a team solution. A creative process of weaving separate threads and loose ends together into a whole.
Accepting while rejecting 'Mike's proposal is an interesting and helpful one, but it would take us rather too long so we must leave it on one side for the present.'	You are accepting Mike, but rejecting his plan in a gracious way. He will not be resentful, and may come up with the winning idea next time.

only general guidance that can be given is to keep it *as simple as possible*. But there is one aspect of planning to which experienced leaders tend to devote more attention than others – contingency planning.

No one can ever make a perfect plan. You cannot foresee every eventuality. Once thinking stops and committee action begins – the real 'point of no return' in decision making – there are bound to be some contingencies – things that happen by chance or through unforeseen causes which affect what you are doing.

A good plan will make some provision for the contingent in human affairs. A prudent householder usually keeps a bit of money in reserve in case some of the things that are liable to happen actually do so. A wise general also keeps a reserve corps available in case the enemy does something he had not expected. You should build a certain amount of flexibility into your plan so that you are not caught out by unforeseen (but not improbable) happenings.

To repeat the point, a good leader thinks ahead. He or she uses their imagination in a disciplined way to picture those contingencies. Their imagination is like a mental radar screen. Once a possible contingency has been picked up they must estimate the chances of it occurring and make provision accordingly. Thus, you have to become an educated guesser. 'All the business of war, and indeed all the business of life', said the Duke of Wellington to a friend over dinner one evening, 'is to endeavour to find out what you don't know by what you do. That's what I called guessing what was at the other side of the hill.' In the language of leadership qualities this is known as *foresight* – seeing what others cannot see because they are not tall enough to look over the hill.

SUMMARY

Planning is a key activity in any working group or organization, and it constitutes one of the principles of leadership.

Once the task has been defined the first step in planning is to search for alternatives. More often than not this work is best done in consultation with others. It is important not only to remain open to, but also to actively encourage, new ideas or possibilities. You should aim to become a **creative thinker** yourself and learn how to stimulate creative or innovative ideas in the group and in each individual.

No plan, however original, is perfect. Indeed, experience tends to teach us that any plan – even if it is a good one – will have a tendency to go off the rails. It is certainly not wise to plan projects on 'best case' scenarios. There should be tolerances or fallback strategies. Glitches – unexpected problems or malfunctions – will occur. So the leader with practical wisdom acts in the knowledge *that there are a number of things that can go wrong.* Not all of these possibilities can be foreseen. Always plan for foreseeable contingencies. If you are flexible you can adjust to your plan any new factors in the situation as they arise. As a French general once said to me, 'A plan is a very good basis for changing your mind.'

Thus, as a planner, you should be developing the necessary abilities for **sharing decision making** where feasible, as well as **creative imagination** and **foresight.** To these should be added, of course, the necessary professional knowledge and technical skills required in your particular work.

> *Adventure is just bad planning.*
>
> Roald Amunsden, Arctic explorer,
> first man to reach the North Pole.

CHECKLIST:
PLANNING YOUR WORK

	Yes	No
Have you listened to specialist advice before making your plan?	☐	☐
Did you consider all the feasible courses of action and weigh them up in terms of resources needed/ available and outcomes?	☐	☐
Have you a programme now which will achieve your objective?	☐	☐
Is there a provision for contingencies?	☐	☐
Did you and the team actively search for a more creative solution as the basis for your plan?	☐	☐
Have you made the plan as simple and as foolproof as possible, rather than complicated?	☐	☐
Does the plan include any necessary preparation or training of the team or individuals?	☐	☐

8

BRIEFING

*'To know how to do it is simple,
the difficulty is doing it.'*
Chinese proverb

The pilots and aircrew shuffle in their chairs and talk among themselves. Outside the rain beats down on the large Nissen hut that serves as a conference room. At 10.00 hours promptly the adjutant calls the room to attention and General Savage strides in and takes his position in the centre of the low platform, feet apart and facing the audience. 'There will be a practice mission this morning. That's right – practice. Our strike photographs show that we haven't been hitting the target lately.'

This is a scene from the Second World War film *Twelve O'Clock High*, which starred Gregory Peck, showing the first meeting of the 918 Bomb Group called by their new commanding officer. It is a film I know exceptionally well as it served as a case study in the two-day functional leadership or action-centred leadership courses that I pioneered. It still remains the feature film that best illustrates the nature and practice of leadership, especially in the military context.

Such briefing sessions are held in all kinds of other organizations, albeit without the drama of a wartime situation. In them the leader is performing a basic leadership function – *briefing the team*. He or she is informing or instructing them thoroughly in advance – in advance, that is, of the action required of them.

The *content* of such a briefing meeting is the result of carrying out two previous functions: defining the task and planning. After stating the objectives and why they are important you have to describe the plan – in outline first and then in greater detail (although this second activity can be delegated to a subordinate or colleague, as General Savage does in the film). It is essential for you to answer the question which will be in everyone's minds, 'What is my part going to be?' So, before and after such a briefing meeting, ask yourself questions such as:

- Does everyone know exactly what his or her job is?
- Has each member of the group clearly defined targets and performance standards agreed between them and me?

The main purpose of a briefing meeting is to allocate tasks to groups and individuals, to distribute resources and to set or check standards of performance. Each person should know at the end what is expected of them and how the contribution of their subgroup or their own efforts will fit in with the purposeful work of everyone else.

EFFECTIVE SPEAKING

A consideration of the leader's method brings us to what are sometimes called vaguely **communication skills**. Here, obviously, you are faced with the need to master the specific ability to speak effectively. How do you do it?

To begin with the good news, you do not have to become

a great orator. You should not concern yourself with the tricks of rhetoric, the techniques taught to would-be demagogues in ancient Athens. The only test is whether or not you can speak in such a way that you *move the group to the desired action*. Demosthenes said to a rival orator: 'You make the audience say, "How well he speaks!" I make them say, "Let us march against Philip!"'

An element of persuasion, in the sense of explaining why in a convincing way, will enter into most briefing or communication meetings. But it will happen more naturally if you have mastered the skills of speaking or briefing. We can identify five sets of skills involved in briefing a group effectively for action. These skills are set out in the table opposite, together with some examples of how to do it.

BRIEFING AND GROUP WORK

Briefing sessions or conferences – work meetings – allow you to do some valuable work in all three areas of the Three Circles model, making general points connected with the specific matter in hand. In the *task* area, for example, you can make it the occasion (as General Savage did) for taking charge. A certain amount of assertiveness is often required of leaders and the group will accept it – even welcome it – if the situation calls for it. You can stress the *team* approach to the task in hand, thus building up team spirit. You can meet *individual* needs by listening to and acknowledging the help of those who help you to achieve the ends of the meeting. The session can also be an opportunity for emphasizing the significance of each individual's contribution to the success of the enterprise.

General Savage in the film was using the medium of the briefing meeting – called for the purpose of informing and instructing – to convey or share his vision, standards or values.

BRIEFING SKILLS		
SKILL	**DEFINITION**	**HOW YOU CAN DO IT**
Preparing	The ability to think ahead and plan your communication.	Give a beginning, middle and end in your talk. Prepare good visual aids, not too many. Arrange the room in advance.
Clarifying	The ability to be clear and understandable.	Unravel the difficulties in your own mind first. Avoid obscure ways of putting things. Seek clarifying questions.
Simplifying	The ability to render complex matters into their simple forms.	Relate the unfamiliar to the familiar with homely analogies. Avoid complicated terminology. Give an overview or outline first. Summarize.
Vivifying	The ability to make a subject come alive.	Use vivid language or methods, even gimmicks. Be enthusiastic and aim to enthuse the group. Use humour if possible.
Being yourself	The ability to cope with nerves and to behave naturally in front of an audience.	Breathe deeply. Eliminate nervous habits. Bear yourself well.

Some of the supreme examples of leadership occur when a leader take over a demoralized group and 'turns it around'. The initial briefing meeting can be especially important in this process. For first impressions are as basic in working relationships as they are in our personal lives.

The impression you make on people at that first meeting will stay with them forever. The task may have to be covered in general terms if you are new to the job – you can do little more than share your first thoughts. But you can share your vision, your spirit of resolve and your determination to change the climate and standards of the group. In a word, you can communicate your spirit – you can inspire. That may entail some tough talking, and people will wait to see if this is going to be backed up by equally firm deeds.

Read this case study in the art of briefing, and then work through the exercise at the end.

On 13 August 1942 Montgomery arrived at Eighth Army Headquarters, two months before the battle of Alamein. 'The atmosphere was dismal and dreary,' he wrote in his diary. That evening he addressed the entire staff of Army Headquarters, between fifty and sixty officers. As he was their fourth Army Commander within a year, he faced a sceptical audience. They plainly doubted if he was the man to reverse their recent defeats and failures. If the morale of that broken army was to be recreated, their hearts had to be won that evening.

Montgomery stood on the steps of his predecessor's caravan and bade the gathering sit on the sand. He spoke without notes, looking straight at his audience.

'I want first of all to introduce myself to you. You do not know me. I do not know you. But we have got to work together, therefore we must understand each other and we must have confidence in each other. I have only been here a few hours. But from what I have seen and heard since I arrived I am prepared to say, here and now, that I have confidence in you. We will then work together as a team, and together we will gain the confidence of this great army and go forward to final victory in Africa.

I believe that one of the first duties of a commander is to create what I call "atmosphere", and in that atmosphere, his staff, subordinate commanders and troops will live and work and fight.

I do not like the general atmosphere I find here. It is an atmosphere of doubt, of looking back to select the next place to which to withdraw, of loss of confidence in our ability to defeat Rommel, of desperate defence measures by reserves in preparing positions in Cairo and the Delta. All that must cease. Let us have a new atmosphere.

The defence of Egypt lies here in Alamein and on the Ruweisat Ridge. What is the use of digging trenches in the Delta? It is quite useless; if we lose this position we lose Egypt; all the fighting troops now in the Delta must come here at once, and will. Here we will stand and fight; there will be no further withdrawal. I have ordered that all plans and instructions dealing with further withdrawal are to be burnt at once. We will stand and fight here.

If we can't stay here alive, then let us stay here dead.

I want to impress on everyone that the bad times are over. Fresh divisions from the UK are now arriving in Egypt, together with ample reinforcements for our present divisions. We have 300 to 400 Sherman new tanks coming and these are actually being unloaded at Suez now. Our mandate from the Prime Minister is to destroy the Axis forces in North Africa; I have seen it written on half a sheet of notepaper. And it will be done. If anyone here thinks it can't be done, let him go at once; I don't want any doubters in this party. It can be done, and it will be done; beyond any possibility of doubt.

Now I understand that Rommel is expected to attack at any moment. Excellent. Let him attack.

I would sooner it didn't come for a week, just to give me time to sort things out. If we have two weeks to prepare we will be sitting pretty; Rommel can attack as soon as he likes after that, and I hope he does.

Meanwhile, we ourselves will start to plan a great offensive; it will be the beginning of a campaign which will hit Rommel and his army for six right out of Africa.

But first we must create a reserve corps, mobile and strong in armour which we will train out of the line. Rommel has always had such a force in his Afrika Corps, which is never used to hold the line but which is always in reserve available for striking blows. Therein has been his great strength. We will create such a corps ourselves, a British Panzer Corps; it will consist of two armoured divisions and one motorized division; I gave orders yesterday for it to begin to form, back in the Delta.

I have no intention of launching our great attack until we are completely ready. There will be pressure from many quarters to attack soon; I will not attack until we are ready and you can rest assured on that point.

Meanwhile, if Rommel attacks while we are preparing, let him do so with pleasure; we will merely continue with our own preparations and we will attack when we are ready and not before.

I want to tell you that I always work on the chief-of-staff system. I have nominated Brigadier de Guingand as Chief-of-Staff Eighth Army. I will issue orders through him. Whatever he says will be taken as coming from me and will be acted on at once. I understand there has been a great deal of 'belly aching' out here. By 'belly aching' I mean inventing poor reasons for not doing what one has been told to do.

All this is to stop at once.

I will tolerate no belly-aching. If anyone objects to

doing what he is told, then he can get out of it; and at once. I want that made very clear right down through the Eighth Army.

I have little more to say just at present. And some of you may think it is quite enough and may wonder if I am mad. I assure you I am quite sane.

I understand there are people who often think I am slightly mad; so often that I now regard it as rather a compliment.

All I have to say to that is that if I am slightly mad, there are a large number of people I could name who are raving lunatics.

What I have done is to get over to you the "atmosphere" in which we will now work and fight; you must see that that atmosphere permeates right down through the Eighth Army to the most junior private soldier. All the soldiers must know what is wanted; when they see it coming to pass, there will be a surge of confidence throughout the army.

I ask you to give me your confidence and to have faith that what I have said will come to pass.

There is much work to be done. The orders I have given about no further withdrawal will mean a complete change in our dispositions; also that we must begin to prepare for our great offensive.

The first thing to do is to move our HQ to a decent place where we can live in reasonable comfort and where the army staff can all be together and side by side with the HQ of the Desert Air Force. This is a frightful place here, depressing, unhealthy and a rendezvous for every fly in Africa; we shall do no good work here. Let us get over there by the sea where it is fresh and healthy. If officers are to do good work they must have decent messes, and be comfortable. So off we go on the new line.

The Chief-of-Staff will be issuing orders on many

points very shortly, and I am always available to be consulted by the senior officers of the staff. The great point to remember is that we are going to finish with this chap Rommel once and for all. It will be quite easy. There is no doubt about it.

He is definitely a nuisance. There we will hit him a crack and finish with him.'

Montgomery stepped down and the officers rose and stood to attention. 'One could have heard a pin drop if such a thing were possible in the sand of the desert,' recollected Montgomery. 'But it certainly had a profound effect, and a spirit of hope, anyway of clarity, was born that evening.' His Chief-of-Staff, de Guingand, agreed: 'It was one of his greatest efforts,' he wrote. 'The effect of the address was electric – it was terrific! And we all went to bed that night with new hope in our hearts, and a great confidence in the future of our Army. I wish someone had taken it down in shorthand, for it would have become a classic of its kind.' Fortunately, it *was* taken down in shorthand and filed away for many years before appearing in print for the first time in 1981.

EXERCISE 7: Montgomery's Alamein address

- How did Montgomery set about changing the group atmosphere?
- What was the common objective he communicated?
- What was the new outline plan?
- Did he set any new group standards?
- What did he expect from all present?
- How did he respond to the individual needs of the staff?
- If you had to choose one word to summarize Montgomery's message, what would it be?

BRIEFING THE INDIVIDUAL

Briefing individuals – giving both information and instructions – is a perennial function of leadership. Like all functions it can be done well, in which case it becomes a skill; or it can be done badly, in which case it is called a disaster. In a crisis or an emergency, those instructions are usually given as commands or orders. In the absence of that life-or-death element or obvious shortage of time, it is best to give instructions in the form of suggestions or questions. Where possible give reasons for the action.

> Tony, I suggest you get that report about sales in France to the marketing director by next Friday, not the following Tuesday. I know he needs it for a Board meeting on Monday. Can you do that, please?

From an early age I noticed that I tended to do things much more willingly if my parents or teachers *asked* me nicely, rather than told me. That may be a personal idiosyncrasy, or an English one. My impression, however, is that most people react in the same way. That is why an element of natural courtesy should flavour all that a leader does. Certainly I have noticed that good leaders tend to ask you to do things – they do not boss you about.

Clearly performing the briefing function with understanding and skill takes you well beyond the specific example of giving instructions to your team before tackling an objective. In the wider context it involves a sustained attempt in the group or organization to let people know what is going on and to create or build a spirit of positive, constructive and confident teamwork.

A short course on leadership

The six most important words: 'I admit I made a mistake.'
The five most important words: 'I am proud of you.'
The four most important words: 'What is your opinion?'
The three most important words: 'If you please.'
The two most important words: 'Thank you.'
The one most important word: 'We.'
And the least most important word: 'I.'

SUMMARY

Perhaps the word most closely associated with leadership in people's minds is **communication**. A good leader communicates. But it is important for you to become more specific than that. In this chapter we have looked at the *briefing* function. That apparently simple activity does call for a number of skills that can be developed.

At the first level of leadership you should strive to become competent at briefing your group on objectives and plans. At the senior level you will have to brief the organization, a much more demanding task. At all levels there are individuals who need to be briefed in clear and simple language. Such occasions – team, organizational or individual – are not to be seen merely in terms of the task. They are also opportunities for you to create the right **atmosphere**, to promote **teamwork**, and to get to know, encourage and motivate each **individual** person.

CHECKLIST:
BRIEFING

	Yes	No
Do you regularly brief your team on the organization's current plans and future developments?	☐	☐

How would you rate yourself on each of the following five skills of briefing effectively?:

	Good	Adequate	Weak
Preparing	☐	☐	☐
Clarifying	☐	☐	☐
Simplifying	☐	☐	☐
Vivifying	☐	☐	☐
Being yourself	☐	☐	☐

In what specific ways can you improve your skills?

1.

2.

3.

Can you identify the most effective briefing talk by a strategic leader that you have ever heard? In one sentence, why was it effective?

	Yes	No
Could your organization improve its two-way communication of information and instructions with those responsible for carrying them out? If so, how?	☐	☐

9

CONTROLLING

**'The hunter in pursuit of an elephant does
not stop to throw stones at birds.'**

African proverb

'No one will miss this bag of gold if I slip it under the table.
In the account I'll put it down as travel expenses.' In the
Middle Ages the royal servants in the various departments of
state were not above helping themselves from the till. Hence,
it was necessary to supervise their accounts of payments and
receipts by keeping a duplicate roll. Then you could check
or verify payments *contra rotulus*, against that (second) roll.
A contraction of this medieval Latin phrase has given us our
modern world *control*. In its wider sense, 'controlling' means
checking and directing action once work has started to
implement the plan. And in this context the primary function of controlling also includes **coordinating** team efforts
and **harmonizing** relations as work proceeds.

At the outset you have to establish that you are in charge.
Then you have to maintain that control. Again, that does
not mean that you will do all the leadership work yourself.
But in their eagerness to help there is always a danger that a
subgroup or an individual team member will in effect take

over control from you. Such specialists or strong individuals can be given their heads on occasion, but you should keep the reins firmly in your own hands. However quiet you may be by nature, you must not allow anyone to dominate you or the group. Brave self-assertion is needed. Timidity is out. It is fatal to authority if you give instructions (as orders, suggestions or questions) and then act like a small boy who throws a stone and runs away.

Once work has started on a project it is vitally important that you *control* and *coordinate* what is being done, so that everyone's energy is turning wheels and making things happen – or most of the group's energy anyway, for human beings are as inefficient as old steam engines and steam is always escaping one way or another. But *most* of that synergy or common energy of the group should be fully deployed in implementing the common plan and producing the desired results.

How do you do it? The secret of controlling is to have a clear idea in your mind of what should be happening, when it should occur, who should be doing it and how it should be done. The more effectively you have involved the group in your planning the more likely it is that they too will have a similar clear picture of what is required. The ideal is that the team or the individual with whom you are dealing should become self-controlling, so as to regulate its own performance against standards or the clock. 'We have only got two hours left, so we will have to work harder to get the job done to meet the deadline.' Your aim as a leader is to intervene as little as possible.

A leader is best
When people barely know that he exists.
Not so good when people obey and acclaim him,
Worst when they despise him.

'Fail to honour people,
They fail to honour you';
But of a good leader, who talks little
When his work is done, his aim fulfilled,
They will all say, 'We did this ourselves.'

Lao-Tzu, Sixth century BC

Your object, then, in directing, regulating and restraining is to ensure that the group's work keeps within bounds or remains on course like a ship at sea. That is the sole criterion of your effectiveness as a controller. You have oversight, which means you should be able to look at the whole picture. If obstacles or difficulties crop up in the path of the adopted course, you are then in a good position to help the group to cope with them.

The stance of a controller is to be where the action is, but observing rather than doing. If you watch a good leader in the execution phase of an exercise or project, his or her eyes are never still. The pattern of ability here is: **look**, **think**; and **intervene** only where strictly necessary and with the minimum exercise of power.

Obviously if a safety standard is being ignored and someone is in danger of losing life or limb, your thought processes will be instant. But much of what you pick up on will be below-standard performance (especially if you are inclined to be a perfectionist), and you will have to make a judgement as to whether to intervene immediately or to make the points later.

If you decide on intervention, the principle is to use the minimum force possible. If you are at the controls of an ocean-racing yacht, for example, you do not normally have to force the rudder about or lunge around at the crew with a boathook. In order to get the group onto its agreed course again you may only have to touch the controls – a quiet word or even a look can do the trick. As the Arabs say, 'Who does not understand a look cannot understand long explanations.' The personal course you have to steer as a leader should take you between the two black rocks of *too much interference* and *lack of direction*. Many a leader is shipwrecked in these foaming straits.

If the plan is going well and the group is composed of self-disciplining people, you can sometimes have time to help an individual or a subgroup with their part of the task. If you want everyone to work hard you must not give the impression that you are standing around with nothing to do. Yet you should always remain in such a position that you can instantly take control if things begin to go wrong. Some leaders make the mistake of getting so involved in a piece of work that they forget their responsibility for the whole. You do not see the whole forest if you are busy cutting down a tree – which your woodman could do better than you if only he could get his hands on *his* axe! Setting an example of hard work is always a good idea, as long as it does not detract from your function as director and controller.

CONTROLLING A MEETING

Taking the chair in committees and at meetings is a leadership role. Therefore the Three Circles model applies. Decision making is essential too, because that is usually what meetings and committees are about. Consequently there is relatively little to be added specifically about the chairperson's job providing you have grasped the elements of good leadership. What matters most then is to observe and learn from experienced chairmen or chairwomen at work. They are rare people, and you should not miss the opportunity of watching closely how they conduct a meeting so that the tasks are achieved, the group works as a team and each individual contributes effectively according to their talents.

There are some leadership functions needed more frequently in committees and meetings than elsewhere. The skill of silencing people in a firm but friendly way has to be developed. The skill of testing for consensus is also vital. A good chairperson will sense that area of consensus, which is rather like the invisible ever-moving centre of a shoal of fish. Here, his or her ability to read non-verbal behaviour – a raised eyebrow, a half-smile, a vigorous nod – can be significant. If you watch a good leader in the chair you will notice that he or she always keeps an eye upon the faces of the committee members. Lastly, the skill of summarizing may have to be employed more than once during a meeting. It is a means of taking bearings, to ensure that the ship is still on course.

Controlling the Cabinet

The Cabinet usually meets once a week. That should be enough for regular meetings, and should be if they grasp from the start what they are there for. They should be back at their work as soon as possible, and a Prime Minister should put as little as possible in their way. We started sharp at 11, and rose in time for lunch. Even in a crisis, another couple of meetings should be enough in the same week: if there is a crisis, the less talk the better.

The Prime Minister shouldn't speak too much himself in Cabinet. He should start the show or ask somebody else to do so, and then intervene only to bring out the more modest chaps who, despite their seniority, might say nothing if not asked. And the Prime Minister must sum up. Experienced Labour leaders should be pretty good at this; they have spent years attending debates at meetings of the Parliamentary Party and the National Executive, and have to sum *those* up. That takes some doing – good training for the Cabinet.

Particularly when a non-Cabinet Minister is asked to attend, especially if it is his first time, the Prime Minister may have to be cruel. The visitor may want to show how good he is, and go on too long. A good thing is to take no chance and ask him to send the Cabinet a paper in advance. The Prime Minister can then say, 'A very clear statement, Minister. Do you need to add anything?' In a firm tone of voice obviously expecting the answer, *No.* If somebody else looks like making a speech, it is sound too nip in with 'Has anybody any objection?' If somebody starts to ramble, a quick, 'Are you *objecting*? You're not? Right. Next business,' and the Cabinet can move on.

It is essential for the Cabinet to move on, leaving in its wake a trail of clear, crisp, uncompromising decisions. This is what government is about. And the challenge to democracy is how to get it done quickly.

Clement Attlee

CONTROLLING IN ORGANIZATIONS

In organizations as opposed to groups it is essential that some *control systems* are established, for a leader at the top cannot obviously do all the controlling themselves. What the strategy leader has to do in concert with the senior leadership team is to ensure that leaders at all levels are carrying out the controlling function. In order to control, a controlling system of checks has to be introduced to give the necessary information. Successful organizations are characterized by both delegation of the controlling function right down to the frontline, and also by some set of central controlling systems.

Rolleron, a firm making garden tools and machinery, really took off when it bought Clive Mitchell's invention of a lawnmower capable of self-sharpening. The machine was also especially resistant to stones damaging the blades and throwing them out of true.

Within three years the firm had grown from 300 to 3000 employees. But the top leadership failed to introduce a proper system of annual budgeting, with monthly checks against the target figures. Costs rose; debts mounted. The company's board did not receive information in time of a slight down-turn in the lawnmower market, which would have allowed them to switch resources to other areas.

A cash flow problem proved to be the straw which broke the camel's back. 'A company with an excellent produce and willing staff,' said the public receiver in his report on its bankruptcy. 'But its management failed to establish proper financial controls.'

That story is by no means unique. The one characteristic that almost all companies that fail possess is *poor two-way communication in the controlling function*. At whatever level you are operating as a leader, you have to direct and control the situation – or it will control you.

SELF-CONTROL

If you cannot control yourself you are unlikely to be able to control others. Take bad temper as an example. An occasional explosion of anger does no harm if the provocation is evident and treatable. Leaders tend not to be placid, and the capacity for justified anger is important. Your people should be wary of getting on the wrong side of you by being wilfully inefficient or ineffective. But bad temper is a very different matter. It is far from being a harmless weakness, a mere matter of temperament. If you are easily ruffled, quick-tempered or 'touchy' by disposition, people will diagnose it as caused by a lack of patience, kindness, courtesy or unselfishness.

Remember, however, that all your weaknesses are merely tendencies to act in a certain way. They do not guarantee that you will do so. Hundreds of leaders have successfully curbed their fiery tempers, harnessing the energy released rather than allowing it to simply 'blow their top'. 'Leaders', said Paul of Tarsus, 'should not be "easily provoked".'

There are plenty of other aspects in us that invite self-control. Just controlling your tongue – that unruly member – can be a formidable job. The encouraging fact is that each small victory over one of these tendencies makes the next encounter a little easier. As Shakespeare wrote in *Hamlet*:

> *Refrain tonight,*
> *And that shall lend a kind of easiness*
> *To the next abstinence, the next more easy;*
> *For use almost can change the stamp of nature.*

CALM, COOL AND COLLECTED

There are some situations which naturally invite fear or anxiety. Everyone must be aware that fear is contagious. Just as an animal can smell or sense whether or not you are afraid of it, so can people. You only have to recall how panic can suddenly seize a crowd without a word being spoken. But courage – the resource in us which enables us to contain or overcome fear – is also contagious.

Being human, you will have as much fear and anxiety as anyone else in the group or organization. But fear paralyses.

If you want the group to continue working then fear has to be neutralized. If you can calm yourself, remaining a still centre in the storm, that calmness will be radiated to others. 'If you can keep your head when those about you are losing theirs and blaming it on you', as Kipling wrote. If you can do that, then people will calm down and begin to think and work constructively.

Sometimes a calm leader's appearance on the scene can change the situation. In his novel *Typhoon* Joseph Conrad graphically describes the relief of a first mate in a severe gale: 'Jukes was uncritically glad to have his captain at hand. It relieved him as though that man had, by simply coming on deck, taken at once most of the gale's weight upon his shoulders. Such is the prestige, the privilege, and the burden of command.' Compare the Arab proverb: 'A frightened captain makes a frightened crew.'

In his Cabinet room when he was Prime Minister, Harold Macmillan kept a card in front of him with this sentence in his own handwriting: 'Quiet, calm deliberation disentangles every knot.' That is a good practical rule of thumb for a leader to follow.

Military history gives us some vivid examples of great leadership in this respect. I think of General Robert E. Lee at Gettysburg when he knew the battle was lost. As one officer beside him in that dark hour wrote: 'His face did not show the slightest disappointment, care or annoyance, and he addressed to every soldier he met a few words of encouragement. "All will come right in the end, we'll talk it over afterwards." And to a Brigade Commander speaking angrily of the heavy losses of his men: "Never mind, General, all this has been my fault. It is I who have lost this fight, and you must help me out of it the best way you can."'

My own favourite example comes from Napoleon's disastrous Russian campaign. On the retreat from Moscow in that terrible winter of 1812 the Emperor entrusted the command of the rearguard – the most hazardous post of all – to Marshal Ney. At one point the rearguard found itself under constant attack by the Russian forces. They sustained heavy losses; they were starving, short of ammunition and freezing in the bitter cold. According to Ney's aide-de-camp, Colonel De Frezenac, their position seemed utterly hopeless.

But the presence of Marshal Ney was enough to reassure us. Without knowing what he intended or what he could do, we knew that he would do something. His confidence in himself was equal to his courage. The greater the danger, the more prompt was his resolution, and once he had decided on what course to take he never doubted of success. Thus, even at a moment like this, his face showed no sign of indecision or anxiety. Everyone turned his eyes to him, but no one ventured to question him. At last, seeing one of his staff near him, the Marshal said in a low voice:

'It is not well with us.'

'What are you going to do?' replied the officer.

'Get to the other side of the Dnieper.'

'Where is the way to it?'

'We shall find out.'

'But what if it is not frozen over?'

'It will be.'

When they reached the Dnieper the French soldiers managed to get across the frozen river but the ice was not thick enough to bear the weight of their train of cannons. One of Ney's staff officers fell through the ice and Ney himself crawled on his hands and knees to haul him out. In the language of this book, despite the immense burden of his responsibilities for *task* and *team*, Ney found time for the need of an *individual*. When Napoleon later heard of Ney's exploits in the retreat from Moscow he commented, 'Ney is the bravest of the brave.'

SUMMARY

The function of **controlling** involves checking against standards and directing the course of work in progress. **Coordinating** and **harmonizing** implies that you as leader are watching the team at work, poised to intervene constructively if the need arises, and ensuring that the team is working as a team at its best.

That does not mean you should have no work of your own or never lend a hand. But primarily your responsibility for the whole team effort should come first. If you have performed the foregoing functions well and trained your team, it should become largely **self-controlling.**

Meetings in particular call for skilled control by the chairperson.

The power of your physical presence is especially important when things are either going wrong or when there is a danger of that happening and it is all falling apart. At such times what is needed is a positive climate. Your spirit – your calmness – will communicate itself to the group. You can inspire confidence. Make your decision and brief the group on what is to be done. Remember that in such crisis situations almost any decision is better than none.

Controlling implies more than simply being firmly in charge. In organizations it is essential to set up **control systems**, which should be kept as simple as possible. Most organizations that fail exhibit – among other things – poor financial controls.

It is useless to seek to control others if you cannot control yourself. 'In managing human affairs', said Lao-Tzu, 'there is no better rule than self-restraint.' That implies not only such things as controlling your use of time but also managing your emotions so that they do not take control of you. Fear or anxiety, anger or impatience: these are your unruly lodgers that you should keep under lock and key.

Ergomet sum mihi imperatum
('I am myself my own commander')

Plautus (Roman playwright)

CHECKLIST:
CONTROLLING

	Yes	No
Do you maintain a balance between controlling with too tight a rein and giving the group too much freedom to do as it pleases?	☐	☐
Are you able to coordinate work in progress, bringing all the several parts into a common, harmonious action in proper relation to each other?	☐	☐
On those occasions when you are directly involved with the 'technical' work, do you make arrangements so that the team requirements and the specific needs of its members are not ignored or overlooked?	☐	☐

What were the three characteristics of the most effective chairman or chairwoman of meetings you have come across?

1. ....

2. ....

3. ....

When you are 'in the chair', do meetings run over the time
allotted for them?:

Never ☐   Sometimes ☐   Always ☐

Is the organization you work for noted with customers on
account of its control systems in the following areas?:

Quality of product/service ☐

Delivery ☐

Keeping costs down ☐

Safety ☐

10

EVALUATING

'If you can meet with Triumph and Disaster
And treat those two imposters just the same . . .'
Rudyard Kipling

Appraising, evaluating, reviewing, rating, assessing, judging and estimating are all aspects of the basic function of valuing. These ships can all sail here under the flagship of *evaluating*: the ability to determine or fix the value of something.

Like analysing and synthesizing, the other two basic functions of intelligence, valuing enters into all of a leader's thinking and action. The controlling function, for example, clearly involves some evaluating of progress against yardsticks or standards. In this section we will concentrate on some specific skills which you will need to acquire or develop as a leader, namely:

- Assessing consequences
- Evaluating team performance
- Appraising and training individuals
- Judging people.

On judgement

Judgement is necessary because the Cabinet is the instrument by which the decisions are reached with a view to action, and decisions stem from judgement. A Cabinet is not a place for eloquence – one reason why good politicians are not always good Cabinet Ministers. It is judgement which is needed to make important decisions on imperfect knowledge in a limited time. Men either have it, or they haven't. They can develop it, if they have it, but cannot acquire it if they haven't.

Strength of character is required to stand up to criticism from other Cabinet members, pressure from outside groups, and the advice of civil servants.

It is also necessary when policies on which the Cabinet has agreed are going through the doldrums, or are beginning to fail. A man of character will neither be, or seem to be, bowed by down by this. Nor will he be blown about by 'every wind of vain doctrine'.

Clement Attlee

ASSESSING CONSEQUENCES

In all organizations there are some people who have a reputation for good judgement, in the sense that they are adept at assessing the consequences of any potential action inside and outside the organization. Equally we all know people who lack judgement in this respect. In industry they are often responsible for triggering off strikes, stoppages or other breakdowns in industrial relations.

In the decision making or problem-solving process you will have to assess the consequences of proposed courses of action or solutions before making up your mind. It is helpful to bear in mind that consequences can be divided into six categories, which overlap considerably. These are described in the table below.

PROBING THE CONSEQUENCES	
TYPE OF CONSEQUENCE	**PROBING QUESTIONS**
Desirable	What solid advantages does this course or solution have in terms of the common purpose, aim or objective?
Undesirable	Does it have unwelcome side effects? Does it create more problems than it solves?
Manifest	What consequences – good or bad – are open to view now?
Latent	There will be consequences I cannot foresee now. Can I cut down their number by further thought or research? Have I sufficient resources to deal with possible contingencies?
Task	What are the technical consequences of adopting this method rather than that?
People	What will be the effects on (a) team (b) individuals (c) organization (d) society (e) myself?

In some instances you will be reduced to rough estimates or guesses about these consequences. But the greater the amount of science you bring to bear, the more you can predict consequences with accuracy. Where possible, turn estimates into calculations. In industry that means carrying out a rigorous cost/benefit evaluation of the courses open to you.

With regard to 'people' consequences – a matter of vital concern to the leader – a common mistake is to guess the consequences instead of finding out by going and asking the people concerned. 'They will never agree to working extra shifts, that's for sure. They never have done in the past', said a board director. But that is an unexamined assumption. (Remember Exercise 5 – the dots and matchsticks!) Test that consequence to see if it is a real one – you may get a pleasant surprise.

Someone once neatly summed up the decision making process as being in three phases: making the decision, implementing it, and living with the consequences. The last phase divides into two forms at the point where you are deciding: **manifest** – plainly apparent or obvious at the time; and **latent** – hidden or concealed to the decision maker.

You can develop your ability to assess those consequences in advance – except for the latent ones – by carefully analysing cause-and-effect in what happens. Gradually you will identify patterns or tendencies. It becomes easier to predict what will happen. Your 'depth mind' – the subconscious centre, or most of your ten thousand million brain cells – can sometimes act as a computer in this respect, printing out warnings, judgements or expectations. An informed or educated depth mind, fed upon experience analysed and digested, is a valuable asset for any leader.

A leader's private computer

If I have any advice to pass on, it is this: if one wants to be successful, one must think until it hurts. One must worry a problem in one's mind until it seems there cannot be another aspect of it that hasn't been considered. Believe me, that is hard work and, from my close observation, I can say that there are few people indeed who are prepared to perform this arduous and tiring work.

But let me go further and assure you of this: while, in the early stages, it is hard work and one must accept it as such, later one will find that it is not so difficult, the thinking apparatus has become trained; it is trained even to do some of the thinking subconsciously. The pressure that one had to use on one's poor brain in the early stages no longer is necessary; the hard grind is rarely needed; one's mental computer arrives at decisions instantly or during a period when the brain seems to be resting. It is only the rare and most complex problems that require the hard toll of protracted mental effort.

Roy Thomson, After I was Sixty (1975)

EVALUATING TEAM PERFORMANCE

In working enterprises it is often valuable to have a 'debriefing' session after a particular project. This gives you the chance to evaluate the performance of the group as a whole in relation to the task. First you should have a realistic and honest statement of results in terms of the following.

Success	Objectives all achieved.
Limited success	Some objectives or part of the objective achieved but not others.
Failure	None of the objectives achieved.

Then you should move on to the evaluation proper. You can either initiate this phase by giving your own views, or invite comments from the team as a whole. Unless you are a very experienced leader, it is best always to follow the simple drill of identifying the good points first – what went well – and then moving on to the points for improvement. These should include constructive ways in which the team performance as a whole can be changed for the better. You may take decisions on the spot to effect these changes or choose to think about it for a day or two.

Group meetings for debriefing purposes are usually not the right place to deal with individual failings unless you want to make an example of someone for the benefit of the group as a whole.

At debriefing meetings, however, you can tackle any particular problems that have caused the group to fragment into independent rather than inter-dependent parts. The film *Twelve O'Clock High* provides a good illustration of the latter. During one debriefing meeting, while the 918 Bomb Group is still sustaining heavy losses over enemy territory, Savage finds that some individuals are putting their close friends first.

SAVAGE: Pettigill!

PETTIGILL: Yes, Sir.

SAVAGE: We were plenty lucky to have only one loss on this strike. Why did you break formation?

PETTIGILL: Well, Sir, Ackermann was in trouble, two engines on fire, and we were getting enemy fighters. I figured I'd better stay back with him and try to cover him going into the target. But he couldn't make it.

SAVAGE: (after a pause) Ackermann a pretty good friend of yours?

PETTIGILL: My room-mate Sir.

SAVAGE   So for the sake of your room-mate, you violated Group integrity. Every gun on a B.17 is designed to give the Group maximum defensive fire-power, that's what I mean by Group integrity. When you pull a B.17 out of formation you reduce the defensive power of the Group by ten guns. A crippled aeroplane has to be expendable. The one thing which is never expendable is your obligation to this Group. This Group, this Group, that has to be your loyalty, your only reason for being! Stovall!

STOVEALL	Yes, Sir.
SAVAGE	Have the Billeting Officer work out a complete reassignment of quarters so that every man has a new room-mate.
STOVEALL	Very well, Sir.

In this scene Savage shows considerable skill which is worth exploring further. He *senses* a problem and asked a *probing question* to complete his diagnosis: 'Is Ackermann a pretty good friend of yours?' He *orders* the reallocation of rooms to deal with what he has diagnosed as a *general problem*, and he *reiterates the group standard* he is trying to set: in this case putting the group first and personal relationships second.

APPRAISING AND TRAINING INDIVIDUALS

'Appraisal meeting' is a familiar term in management jargon. This is a regular interview, sometimes as infrequently as once a year, when a manager sits down with his or her subordinate and appraises the work of the subordinate against their objectives. 'Don't tell me that the man is doing good work.' said Andrew Carnegie to one of his plant bosses. 'Tell me what good work he is doing.'

During an appraisal meeting you should create an environment where you can have a constructive dialogue with a subordinate (or superior or colleague for that matter) on the following agenda:

- Past performance.
- Future work to be done, targets, priorities, standards and strategies.
- Matching perceptions of what each can reasonably expect from the other.
- Improving skill, knowledge and behaviour.

PERFORMANCE APPRAISAL INTERVIEWING		
	GUIDELINES	**NOTES**
1.	Ensure the necessary data is available.	To substantiate discussion and to keep it factual, all documents, reports, data or back-up information should be readily available for the interview.
2.	Put the other person at ease.	Both parties should try to be relaxed, open-minded, aware of the purpose of the meeting, committed to its purpose and prepared to discuss things calmly and frankly.
3.	Control the pace and direction of the interview	Both parties have a part to play to control and influence the pace and direction of the interview to keep it relevant, helpful and work-orientated.
4.	Listen . . . listen . . . listen.	The most difficult part of the interview is for both parties to really listen to each other. Listening is more than not speaking, it is emptying the mind of preconceived ideas or prejudices. It is being willing to consider another person's point of view and, if that view is better than the one previously held, being humble enough – and big enough – to accept it.
5.	Don't be destructively critical.	Where possible, people should be encouraged to be self-critical – critical of their own performance and motivated to improve. This approach goes a long way to removing unnecessary conflict from the meeting.

6.	Review performance systematically.	It is important to stick to the facts – facts which can be substantiated – and that's where the relevant back-up information comes in handy.
7.	Discuss future action.	This is an opportunity to discuss with one another – almost on equal terms – what has been done, how it can best be done, who will do it, when, and to what standard.
8.	Be prepared to discuss potential or aspirations.	The question of the individual's potential for future promotion doesn't always arise, but it is wise to be prepared for it.
9.	Identify essential training/development required.	The final part of the interview is usually devoted to discussing the training and counselling which may be required in order to carry out the agreed action plan.
10.	Avoid obvious pitfalls.	Such things as: • talking too much and hogging the conversation • introducing unnecessary conflict • jumping to hasty conclusions • unjustly blaming others – particularly those who are not present to defend themselves • expecting the impossible – like wanting a person to change significant character traits overnight • lastly, making promises which neither party may be able to keep.

The table on pages 132 and 133 contains some guidelines which you may find useful to both the roles of being an appraiser and of being appraised.

At the end of the meeting or shortly afterwards, any agreed future actions should be written down. What has to be done? When? To what standard?

Do not expect too much from a system of formal performance appraisal meetings. Certainly if they are not followed up by action from both the appraiser and the appraisee they can soon degenerate into empty rituals. But the results of a good appraisal, when linked with good counselling, include better teamwork, improved commitment and the development of knowledge, skill and character.

On-the-job training

General Horrocks recalled one incident which revealed Montgomery's ability to develop the individual, even at the higher levels of leadership.

'On the day after the battle [Alam Haifa] I was sitting in my headquarters purring with satisfaction. The battle had been won and I had not been mauled in the process. What could be better? Then in came a liaison officer from Eighth Army headquarters bringing me a letter in Monty's even hand. This is what he said:

"Dear Horrocks,
Well done – but you must remember that you are now a corps commander and not a divisional commander . . ."

He went on to list four or five things which I had done wrong, mainly because I had interfered too much with the tasks of my subordinate commanders. The purring stopped abruptly.

Perhaps I wasn't quite such a heaven-sent general after all. But the more I thought over the battle, the more I realized that Monty was right. So I rang him up and said, "Thank you very much."

I mention this because Montgomery was one of the few commanders who tried to train the people who worked under him. Who else, on the day after his first major victory, which had altered the whole complexion of the war in the Middle East, would have taken the trouble to write a letter like this in his own hand to one of his subordinate commanders?'

Lieut. General Sir Brian Horrocks, *A Full Life* (1956)

Therefore, you should see the formal system as at best a safety net for a process that should be going on continually. As the leader, you should be continually assessing the value of each individual's contribution and giving him or her feedback on how they are doing. Sometimes individuals, especially the over-modest ones, may genuinely undervalue some action or function they perform. It is a kind of occupational inferiority complex. The leader can correct this misjudgement. He or she may also, as we have seen, have occasion to point out the shortfalls in objectives.

However, a leader is not in the seat of a judge in the law court impartially appraising someone's actions while they stand in the dock. He or she is out to improve performance. Leaders have to be skilled in communicating their perceptions of the strengths and the weaknesses of the individual concerned. They must have data or information at hand to back up any observation they give. Above all, they must put their suggestions across so that they are acceptable and actionable by the individual. The best way to do that is to ask the individual to appraise his or her own performance against standing or continuing aims and specific objectives. Then agree with them an action plan for the future.

Thus, clearly the function of appraising an individual's

performance is only useful if it is the prelude to some form of learning or training. Even if the result of the interview is that you dismiss that person, or transfer him or her to another group, the meeting can still be presented in a positive light as a lesson you have learned together. As a leader you need to be in part a teacher or trainer of people. Conversely, a teacher has to be something of a leader.

It is possible to teach yourself specific techniques, such as asking questions of different kinds which may be useful in appraisal meetings. The following may be useful examples.

Opening	'Tell me about your sales programme.'
Probing	'Is that the first time you failed to meet a target?'
Factual	'Where were you when it happened?'
Reflective	'You obviously feel very disappointed and upset at what was said to you.'
Leading	'I suppose you will improve that next year?
Limited choice	'If you had to choose between general recruitment work and specializing in employment law, which would it be?'

What matters more, however, is to take seriously your responsibilities for developing the individual as his or her mentor throughout the year, not just for an hour or two in a formal or semi-formal meeting. You should be able to offer each individual person something drawn from your practical wisdom.

Unfortunately, unless your subordinate appraises *you* highly in that respect, he or she is unlikely to want to learn from you. As Winston Churchill once remarked to his wife, 'I cannot stand being taught – but I enjoy learning.' What is it in you that might make people want to learn from you? Given that you have a modicum of wisdom, it is best to see yourself not as a coach training a sportsman, but as a more experienced artist sitting down beside another and commenting helpfully on the work in hand.

Remember Cicero's definition of an orator: 'a good man skilled in speaking'. The development of another person may well test your goodness as well as your skill as a teacher. For practical wisdom consists of intelligence, experience and goodness. But mentoring is one of those activities that can make leadership such a rewarding experience.

JUDGING PEOPLE

You may hear it said about some leaders who are outstanding in other respects, 'He is no judge of character. Some of the appointments he has made have been disastrous.'

Conversely, some people – not all leaders – have a natural flair for forming accurate judgements about people and how they are likely to behave in certain situations. If you have some natural ability as a judge, you can develop it by observation, experience and study. It is especially instructive to check appointments made by others in your organization against your own knowledge of that person on the one hand and the requirements of the job on the other. Would you have made that appointment? Did it turn out to be a good, average or weak decision in terms of results?

The practice of having favourites is a dangerous one for leaders on several scores. First, it breaks up team unity. Research has shown that, if an Arctic traveller makes a favourite of one husky among his sledge dogs, the effectiveness of the whole team sharply deteriorates. Secondly, the person you have chosen as your favourite is seen by others as an example of your judgement about people. If others, who know their colleagues better than you do, fail to agree upon your apparently high estimate of your favourite's worth, then your credibility suffers. Thirdly, favourites advance by astutely recognizing and pandering to the social and esteem needs of their bosses. If they sense that you like flattery, they will lay it on with a trowel. Some people are natural courtiers and will vie for your favour with such gifts. In time your judgement can become impaired and you may forget the trivial reasons why you have patronized them – such as their charm or amusing conversation – and you may actually promote them into responsible positions, where they will surely fail.

Assuming that you have remained impartial and even-handed (although it is only human to like some people more than others), the best way to improve your judgements and decisions about people is to take these decisions slowly and work harder at them. There should be times when you actively work on the question by analysing your impressions and discussing them with others, followed by times when you relegate the matter to your subconscious or 'depth mind' for further resolution.

People decisions

Among the effective executives I have had occasion to observe, there have been people who make decisions fast, and people who make them rather slowly. But, without exception, they made personnel decisions slowly and they make them several times before they really commit themselves.

Alfred P. Sloan, Jr., former head of General Motors, the world's largest manufacturing company, was reported never to make a personnel decision the first time it came up. He made a tentative judgement, and even that took several hours as a rule. Then, a few days or weeks later, he tackled the question again, as if he had never worked on it before. Only when he came up with the same name two or three times in a row was he willing to go ahead. Sloan had a deserved reputation for the 'winners' he picked. But when asked about his secret, he is reported to have said: 'No secret – I have simply accepted that the first name I come up with is likely to be the wrong name – and I therefore retrace the whole process of thought and analysis a few times before I act.' Yet Sloan was far from a patient man.

Few executives make personnel decisions of such impact. But all effective executives I have had occasion to observe have learned that they have to give several hours of continuous and uninterrupted thought to decisions on people if they hope to come up with the right answer.

Peter Drucker, *The Effective Executive* (1967)

SELF-EVALUATION

Like other functions, you can apply the principle of evaluating to yourself and your work. Indeed, one major objective for you is to form a clear vision of what *excellence* in leadership means. Then you can appraise your progress in the light of it at regular intervals. For the best way to learn leadership is to do your present job as well as possible and to carefully monitor your own performance. If you can develop the insight to monitor your leadership performance, then even mistakes and failures will yield positive lessons.

In this context you should always evaluate yourself in relation to the generic role – the responsibilities and functions of leadership. Leadership is an other-centred activity, not a self-centred one, and therefore you should avoid any form of self-preoccupation. 'We are to consider our responsibilities,' wrote the great British prime minister of the nineteenth century, Gladstone, 'not ourselves. We are to respect the duties of which we are capable, but not our capabilities simply considered. There is to be no complacent self-contemplation, ruminating upon self. When self is viewed, it must always be in the most intimate connection with its purposes.'

SUMMARY

The ability to evaluate is an important leadership function. In this chapter it has been discussed under four headings: *assessing consequences, evaluating team performance, appraising and training individuals* and *judging people.*

A crucial element in decision making is evaluating the alternatives in terms of their consequences – technical, financial and human.

Unless you can **evaluate team performance** with skill, the people working for you will miss a vital part of the feedback which should be coming their way. The better the team, the more it aspires to excellence, and the more it welcomes constructive criticism.

Appraising the **contribution of individuals** is a continuous activity, part of the process of calling forth the best from people. The higher you have risen as a leader, the more important it is for you to develop good **judgement about people.** Avoid having favourites. The test of your ability in this respect lies in the performance of the people you have appointed. 'By their fruits you shall know them.'

CHECKLIST:
EVALUATING

In assessing the outcome of possible courses of action or solutions, do you take time to consider the consequences for the team and the individual as well as for the task?

Always ☐   Sometimes ☐   Rarely ☐

How do you rate yourself as far as judgement in decision making is concerned?:

Good   Your decisions usually have the predicted   ☐
results, you can foresee consequences and
are rarely surprised at outcomes. Shrewd and
discerning at all times.

Average Your predictions of consequences are   ☐
accurate about half the time. Your common
sense is often proved right.

Weak   Poor judgement often mars your   ☐
performance. You tend to guess too much
what will result from a given decision, and
are frequently wrong.

How would you assess yourself as an appraiser of the work of an individual?:

Good   You hold regular appraisal meetings and do   ☐
quite a lot on a day-to-day basis. You always
support general points with evidence. You
tend always to praise first and criticize
second. Your appraising usually results in
better work performance.

Average Sometimes it seems to work; other times not.   ☐
You find it difficult to hit the right note with
some people. Quite frankly, awkward people,
who don't want to learn, defeat you.

Weak   You lose credibility every time you try to appraise someone. It usually ends up in an argument. You tell them, but they refuse to listen. ☐

What is your record in judging people? In selecting and promoting individuals, which of the following statements characterizes your approach?:

You can always pick a winner, and never consult anyone else or seek specialist advice. ☐

You go by first impressions. Even if you think you are wrong you usually return to them in the end. ☐

You take people-decisions slowly. You like to consult others who know the person, often on a confidential basis. You do not trust your own first thought. ☐

You like to see a person in a variety of different situations before making up your mind. Track record is an important factor to you, more so than psychological tests and the like. ☐

You rarely choose a person on technical grounds alone, unless they are working on their own. You try to see them in the context of being a team leader or member, and judge whether they will get on well with the individuals in that group. ☐

Would you regard your regular evaluation of your own performance as (a) more rigorous (b) less searching or (c) about the same as your evaluation of others?

(a) ☐   (b) ☐   (c) ☐

11

MOTIVATING

*'If you know the nature of water
it is easier to row a boat.'*
Chinese proverb

As a leader you have to be able to get the group and its individual members moving – or keep them moving – in the desired direction. This general ability to move and excite people to action is called *motivation*. The subjects of your motivating activity will be the team and the individual. By extension, especially if you become a strategic leader, it will come to include the organization as well.

Various theories of motivation, based largely on the contributions of Maslow, began to influence industry and management in the late 1950s. Douglas McGregor classically pointed out that managers often operated mainly under one of two sets of contrasting explicit or implicit assumptions about people, which he labelled Theory X and Theory Y. These are outlined in the table on page 144.

McGregor made the point that what we believe about a person can help that person to behave in that way (the 'self-fulfilling prophecy'). If you tell someone you believe that they are bone idle, for example, they will tend to live up to

ASSUMPTIONS ABOUT MAN	
THEORY X	**THEORY Y**
Man dislikes work and will avoid it if he can.	Work is necessary to man's psychological growth. Man wants to be interested in his work and, under the right conditions, he can enjoy it.
Man must be forced or bribed to put out the right effort.	Man will direct himself towards an accepted target.
Man would rather be directed than accept responsibility, which he avoids.	Man will seek, and accept, responsibility under the right conditions. The discipline a man imposes on himself is more effective, and can be more severe, than any imposed on him.
Man is motivated mainly by money. Man is motivated by anxiety about his security.	Under the right conditions man is motivated by the desire to realize his own potential.
Most men have little creativity – except when it comes to getting round management rules!	Creativity and ingenuity are widely distributed and grossly underused.

your prediction. If you have a high regard for them, although that is not strictly justified by the facts, they may well rise to meet your expectations.

Natural leaders have always acted on that assumption of worth. They hold a creative or strategic belief in people, despite evidence to the contrary. 'Trust men and they will be true to you,' said Emerson. 'Treat them greatly and they will show themselves great.'

The Pygmalion effect

In George Bernard' Shaw's *Pygmalion*, Eliza Doolittle explains:
'You see, really and truly, apart from the things anyone can pick up (the dressing and the proper way of speaking and so on), the difference between a lady and a flower girl is not how she behaves, but how she's treated. I shall always be a flower girl to Professor Higgins, because he always treats me as a flower girl, and always will, but I know I can be a lady to you, because you always treat me as a lady, and always will.'

Pygmalion was a sculptor in Greek mythology who carved a statue of a beautiful woman that subsequently was brought to life. George Bernard Shaw's play *Pygmalion* (the basis for the musical hit *My Fair Lady*), has a somewhat similar theme: the essence is that one person, by his effort and will, can transform another person. In the world of management, many executives play Pygmalion-like roles in developing able subordinates and in stimulating their performance. What is the secret of their success? How are they different from managers who fail to develop people?

Another expression of this understanding of man as essentially self-motivating appeared in the work of Frederick Herzberg, another American, who involved himself far more than Maslow in industry. Herzberg's contribution was a significant one to our understanding of leadership.

In the mid-1950s Herzberg and his associates interviewed 203 engineers and accountants in Pittsburg to find out why they found some events in their working lives highly satisfying and others highly dissatisfying. Herzberg divided the factors involved into two types, which he called 'motivators' and 'hygiene' factors. The motivators – outlined in the table on the next page – provided longer-lasting satisfaction to individuals. The hygiene factors, which he listed as including company policy and administration, supervision, interpersonal relations, salary, status, job security, personal life and working conditions, cause us dissatisfaction if they are wrong. But if you give a person more of a hygiene factor you will only either reduce their dissatisfaction or else give them a short-lived sense of satisfaction.

Herzberg's 'two-factor' theory has been the cause of much controversial debate. Like most binary interpretation – black-and-white, 'either-or' pieces of analysis – it achieves the

HERZBERG'S TWO-FACTOR THEORY	
What motivates or satisfies people at work is not the opposite of what demotivates or dissatisfies them. There are two separate sets of factors at work. This list describes those identified by Herzberg as motivators.	
FACTOR	**DEFINITION**
Achievement	Sense of bringing something to a successful conclusion; completing a job; solving a problem; making a successful sale. The sense of achievement is in proportion to the size of the challenge.
Recognition	Acknowledgement of a person's contribution; appreciation of work by company or colleagues; rewards for merit.
Job interest	Intrinsic appeal of job; variety rather than repetition; job holds interest and is not monotonous or boring.
Responsibility	Being allowed to use discretion at work; shown trust by company; having authority to make decisions; accountable for the work of others.
Advancement	Promotion in status or job, or the prospect of it.

appearance of simplicity but only at the cost of sacrificing elements of the more complex truth. Money, for example, cannot be regarded as just a hygiene factor: it can serve as a tangible and necessary expression of recognition in some spheres. Nonetheless, Herzberg has had a powerful influence on the movement to increase job satisfaction at work, a practical application of the wider understanding of individual needs.

Although Herzberg included 'supervision' in his set of hygiene factors – those which cause great dissatisfaction when they are not met or are 'wrong' – he was clearly mistaken on this point. Leadership, a word he did not use, is more than just part of someone's job context: in many instances it is integral to the job itself. You only have to look at his list to see that leaders can play a large part in the 'motivating' factors.

THE FIFTY-FIFTY RULE AND THE EIGHT PRINCIPLES OF MOTIVATING

I came to the conclusion that Maslow, Herzberg and that school of thought are only half right about motivation. *Fifty per cent of our motivation comes from within us as we respond to our internal programme of needs; fifty per cent comes from outside ourselves, especially from the leadership we encounter in life.*

This fifty-fifty rule is not meant to be mathematically accurate; rather, it is indicative of the ever-shifting balance between internal and external influences. From it I have deduced eight principles for leaders who want to motivate others. These are as follows.

Be motivated yourself

As a leader you need to be enthusiastic. You can't light a fire with a dead match! There is nothing so contagious as enthusiasm. Certainly, great designs are not accomplished without enthusiasm. As the Bedouin proverb puts it: 'What comes from your heart is greater than what comes from your hand alone.'

Select people who are highly motivated

It is hard to motivate people who are not motivated already. Therefore look for people who have the seeds of high motivation in them. As Oliver Cromwell once said: 'Give me the red-coated captain who knows what he is fighting for and loves what he knows.' Build your team not from those who talk enthusiastically but from those who show eagerness for the business and steady commitment in their actions.

Treat each person as an individual

Theories and principles apply to the generality of people. You will never know how they apply – even if they apply – to any given individual person unless you observe them and talk to them. You will learn what motivates them, and perhaps also how their pattern of motivation has changed over their lifetime. The Greek dramatist Menander once said, ' "Know thyself" is a good saying, but not in all situations. In many it is better to say "Know others".' As a leader you should aspire to know others. A good shepherd knows his sheep by name. John Steinbeck put it thus: 'No one really knows about other human beings. The best you can do is to suppose that others are like yourself.'

Set realistic and challenging targets

The best people like to be stretched – they welcome feasible but demanding tasks. Don't make life too easy for them! Fortunately, business life provides a series of challenges, enough to keep everyone on their toes. Without toil, trouble, difficulty and struggle there is no sense of achievement. Your skill as a leader is to set and agree goals, objectives or targets that both achieve the task and develop the team and its individual members.

Remember that progress motivates

We all need positive feedback that we are moving in the right direction, for that encourages us to persevere in the face of difficulties. 'I will go anywhere, as long as it is forwards,' says David Livingstone. If you as leader can show to your team – and to each individual member – that progress *is* being made, that in itself will feed the determination to press forward on the path of success.

Create a motivating environment

Leadership calls for social creativity every bit as important and demanding as the artistic creativity of painter, sculptor or composer. You are there to build teamwork, and that is a creative activity. More widely, all leaders in an organization should work together to ensure that it is an interesting, stimulating and challenging place of work. Remember the fifty-fifty principle: about half of our motivation comes from outside ourselves, especially the people around us. Their commitment, passion and stimulating creative minds can awaken the sleeping powers within us. Your job as a leader is to foster that learning and motivating environment.

Provide fair rewards

We have a built-in sense of fairness. It is sometimes not easy to ensure equity in salary and bonuses, but it is important to remember that the perception of unfair rewards does have a demotivating effect on most people – Herzberg was right in that respect. As a general principle, financial (and other) rewards should match the relative value of contribution, according to the market assessment for any particular kind of work.

Give recognition

At best money is a crude measure of the value of work. Is a pop star really worth a thousand times more money than a brain surgeon? A good leader should be swift to show recognition to *all* members of the team or organization, however indirect their contribution is to the overall task. You should work on the principle of 'credit where credit is due'. Where the work of people is valued there is always motivation to do it – and to do it well.

MOTIVATION AND INSPIRATION

If you apply the eight principles described above you will find that you are becoming an inspiring leader. For you will be already going far beyond trying to move people by financial incentives or appeals to fear, those levers which the old-style bosses of yesteryear used to the exclusion of all else. You will be imparting to others your own spirit. Admiral Lord St Vincent once wrote in a letter to his young Captain Nelson: 'I never saw a man in our profession who possessed the magic art of infusing the same spirit into others which inspired their own actions as you do. All agree there is but one Nelson.' Through the ages the true leaders have had that same capacity to inspire willing effort in others.

Leaders who inspire

Xenophon knew from personal experience what it was like to inspire soldiers on campaign, but he was also the first and greatest student of leadership. Here is his composite portrait of the inspiring military leader.

'For some commanders make their men unwilling to work and take risks, disinclined and unwilling to obey, except under compulsion, and actually proud of defying their commander. Yes, and these commanders cause these men to have no sense of dishonour when something disgraceful happens.

Contrast the brave and skilful general with a natural gift for leadership. Let him take over command of these same troops, or of others if you like. What effect has he on them? They are ashamed to do a disgraceful act, think it better to obey and take price in obedience, working cheerfully – each man and all together – when it is necessary to work.

Just as a love of work may spring up in the mind of a private soldier here and there, so a whole army under the influence of a good leader is inspired by love of work and ambition to distinguish itself under the commander's eye. If this is the feeling of the rank and file for their commander, then he is an excellent leader.

So leadership is not a matter of being best with bowl and javelin, nor riding the best horse and being foremost in danger, nor being the most knowledgeable about cavalry tactics. It is being able to make his soldiers feel that they must follow him through fire and in any adventure.

So, too, in private industries the man in authority – the director or manager – who can make the workers eager, industrious and persevering – he is the man who grows the business in a profitable way.

On a warship, when out on the high seas and the rowers

must toil all day to reach port, some rowing masters can say and do the right thing to raise the men's spirits and make them work with a will. Other rowing masters are so lacking in this ability that it takes them twice the time to finish the same voyage. Here they land bathed in sweat, with mutual congratulations, master and oarsmen. There they arrive with dry skin; they hate their master and he hates them.'

Quite how an effective leader so inspires a group of people – even the lowest class of citizens in ancient Athens who manned the oars in their naval galleys – that they become a willing and even enthusiastic team will always be a little mysterious. But it can be done – *you* can do it. And when people are truly inspired, material rewards become irrelevant and the fear of punishment is totally absent. 'You do not need a whip to urge on an obedient horse', the Russian proverb says.

SUMMARY

Human motives have their sources in the deeper needs and values within people. A need that becomes conscious is called a want. A leader can sometimes help the process by which needs are transformed into wants.

To provide the right climate and opportunities for these needs to be met for each individual in the group is possibly the most difficult and certainly the most challenging and rewarding of the leader's tasks.

People are indeed self-motivating, but we all respond well to positive influence in the form of **encouragement** from others. To *encourage* means to give hope, confidence or spirit – and sometimes to give active help as well.

Fifty per cent of our motivation comes from within us, and fifty per cent from outside, especially from good leadership. Therefore, as a leader make sure that you get your fifty per cent right by practising these principles:

- Be motivated yourself
- Select people who are highly motivated
- Treat each person as an individual
- Set realistic and challenging targets
- Remember that progress motivates
- Create a motivating environment
- Provide fair rewards
- Give recognition.

As a leader you should always be ready to support, moderate or encourage your team or the individual whom you touch in the course of a day. In the Zulu language there is a name *abakhwezeli* – it means literally 'the one who keeps the fire going'. It is not a bad definition of the motivating function of a leader.

> *Those who are near will not hide their ability, and those who are distant will not grumble at their toil ... That is what is called being a leader and teacher of men.*
>
> Hsü Tzu

CHECKLIST:
MOTIVATING

	Yes	No
Have you agreed with your team members their main targets and continuing responsibilities, together with standards of performance, so that you can both recognize achievement?	☐	☐
Do you recognize the contribution of each member of the team and encourage other team members to do the same?	☐	☐

In the event of success, do you acknowledge it and build on it? In the event of setbacks, do you identify what went well and give constructive guidance for improving future performance? ☐ ☐

Can you delegate more? Can you give more discretion over decisions and more accountability to a subgroup or individual? ☐ ☐

Do you show to those that work with you that you trust them by, for example, not hedging them around with unnecessary controls? ☐ ☐

Are there adequate opportunities for training and (where necessary) retraining? ☐ ☐

Do you encourage each individual to develop his or her capacities to the full? ☐ ☐

Is the overall performance of each individual regularly reviewed in face-to-face discussion? ☐ ☐

Does financial reward match contribution? ☐ ☐

Do you make sufficient time to talk and listen, so that you understand the unique (and changing) profile of needs and wants in each person, enabling you to work with the grain of nature rather than against it? ☐ ☐

Do you encourage able people with the prospect of promotion within the organization, or – if that is impossible – counsel them to look elsewhere for the next position fitting their merit? ☐ ☐

Can you think of a manager who delegates (a) more effectively (b) less effectively than you do? What are the results in each case?

(a) ☐

(b) ☐

12

ORGANIZING

'The summits of the various kinds of business
are, like the tops of mountains, much more alike
than the parts below – the bare principles are
much the same; it is only the rich variegated
details of the lower strata that so contrast with
one another. But it needs travelling to know that
the summits are the same. Those who live on one
mountain believe that their mountain is wholly
unlike all others.'
Walter Bagehot

Just as there are leaders who prove to be extremely weak as
organizers, especially when they are unwisely promoted to
their 'level of incompetence' in the organization, so there are
some who have a talent for organizing but lack ability in other
major functions. Assuming that you already have the potential
for being a good organizer and some experience in organizations, the aim of this chapter is to sharpen your skills.

Organizing is the function of arranging or forming into a
coherent unity or functional whole. It can mean systematic
planning as well, but that is a function we have already

covered. Here 'organizing' means more the structuring that has to be done if people are to work as a unit with each element performing its proper part. It is essentially concerned with getting right the relation of the whole to the parts. It is a manifestation of perhaps a deep vocational impulse to impose or bring order in place of chaos. Order is the value that lies behind society, just as freedom is the value that lies behind the individual. A balance needs to be struck in any group or organization between order and freedom.

ORGANIZING THE GROUP

In order to achieve anything you may have to give your group some structure, especially if it is large and the task is complex. These structures may be temporary – for the duration of the exercise – or permanent.

If the group in question is a permanent or continuing one, with individuals joining and leaving it, it may well be part of a larger organization. In which case the organization as a whole or your predecessor as leader may already have defined subgroups with leaders. You may wish to maintain that ready-made structure, or introduce changes. The essence of organizing at this level is to break up the group as it gets larger into smaller subgroups and to appoint leaders who are responsible to you.

This will give you a second communications system. The first is the method of talking to the whole group yourself and listening to what they say – two-way, face-to-face communication. The content will include purpose, policies, progress and people. The advantage of this method is that it is not liable to the communication failures which occur when you are passing messages to another person via a third (and fourth and fifth . . .) party. However, it is time-consuming.

Much – but not all – of this communication work can be delegated to sub-leaders. A good and well trained sub-leader will not only pass on and interpret messages accurately, but will also report back to you clearly and concisely the reactions, constructive ideas or suggestions which arose in his or her subgroup meeting on such areas as:

- How to do the *task* more effectively
- How we can work better as a *team*
- How *individuals* can make their optimal contribution.

The structure not only gives you a second communication system, it also provides you with another option in your decision making and problem solving strategy. You can now put a problem to, or ask for proposed courses of action or solutions from, your inner leadership team of subgroup leaders rather than to the group as a whole. In choosing when to use each of these two methods for decision making, it is important to be flexible according to the needs of the situation, the size and character of the group and the kind of decision involved.

If you group is a large one (twenty or more) it is essential to sub-divide it and appoint (or allow the members to elect) leaders responsible to you, otherwise the individual needs described elsewhere in this book are not going to be met. You want each of your sub-leaders to involve their people in the task, develop a team approach and to inspire, encourage and control individuals as necessary. The more the subgroups can take on these functions themselves, with the minimum of supervision, the better. But that, paradoxically, requires good leadership from you and their subgroup leader.

ORGANIZING THE ORGANIZATION

'Organizing the organization' may appear to be a rather meaningless subheading. After all, the organization is by definition the end result of the function of organizing. It is finished, complete and unalterable. Of course it is none of those things in reality, but we tend to make assumption that it is so.

An organization is indeed sometimes the product of another person's organizing activity. These days it is more likely to be a committee who did the organizing.

Some old and venerable kinds of organization, such as churches and armies, have structures which have lasted centuries, modified but essentially unchanged. The fact that they have withstood the test of time may well be evidence that they are sound, but you cannot take that for granted. Whether the structure you are working in is the product of a single leader, a committee or a tradition, you should not assume that it is perfect either in the sense of being completely finished or in the sense of being without serious fault or blemish.

For it is *people* who did the organizing, and they are always fallible. They may have organized, for instance, with a particular interpretation of the enduring purpose in mind, or in light of a given technology, or assuming a certain level of education or training among members of the organization. The *situational* factors are changing and therefore as a leader in an organization you will need to examine the function of organizing in one way or another.

Assuming that the organization is not as hard as concrete but is organic – growing and developing or contracting according to the situation – your organizing ability will be constantly in play, introducing changes or modifications to the system of ways of doing things. From time to time it is advisable to carry out a survey of the structure of the organization.

You do not want to make changes in this basic structure too often, for no organization (like the individual person) can stand too much change all at once. If you make a major organizational change, and get it wrong, you are stuck with the consequences for the next five years – longer, maybe, if it is a very big organization. So it is important to get it right.

Providing you take the Three Circles model as your guide you can undertake this structural survey without too much difficulty, especially if you set up a small but representative steering group to work with you. The key is to ask yourselves the right questions. Some suggestions are outlined in the diagram below and table overleaf.

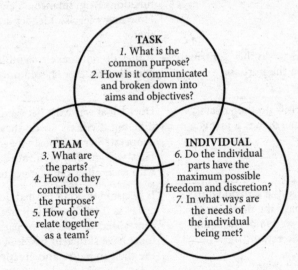

Whether you start at the top and work downwards, or vice versa, it is important to be systematic about it. You are trying to see how the pieces of the jigsaw fit together at

SURVEYING YOUR ORGANIZATION

QUESTION	NOTES
1. What is the common purpose?	Besides studying statements of purpose, look at what the organization is actually doing. How does it spend its time and money?
2. How is it communicated and broken down into aims and objectives?	This should lead you into the communication and decision making processes, vital areas in any organization.
3. What are the parts?	Identify the main groups and subgroups. These are often divided between line (or operations) and staff (or functions), e.g. finance, sales. How many levels of leader are there?
4. How do they contribute to the purpose?	If they do not make a significant contribution they should not be there.
5. How do they relate together as a team?	Does tribal war exist between the different divisions, or do they cooperate harmoniously together? How well do they communicate with each other on a lateral basis?
6. Do the individual parts have the maximum possible freedom and discretion?	Is decision making pushed down as far as it will go, or is it heavily centralized? Do the main parts or units have sufficient freedom to use their initiative and creativity?
7. In what ways are the needs of the individual being met?	This will take you into systems of remuneration, personnel policy and maybe relations with trades unions.

| 8. Do the circles sufficiently overlap? | You will soon find out how far the circles overlap in the minds of employees. Is the overlap sufficient to provide and maintain high morale in spite of difficulties? |
| 9. How are tensions between the three circles resolved? | This will take you into the consultative system, disciplinary procedures and the methods for dealing with disputes. |

present, and to collect and collate ideas on how a better structure and method of working together might look.

At the lowest level you should search out the answers to the question 'How large or small should the primary group or groups be in this industry?' A good guideline is to establish how many people one person can supervise in light of the factors shown in the table above.

The Roman Army, like the Israelites, operated with a primary group of ten soldiers led by a *decanus* (hence our word 'dean'). A football and cricket team consists of eleven players. However simple the task in technological terms, the span of control of a team leader should probably not exceed ten or twelve people. This refers to the number who are directly responsible to any given leader, and who therefore constitute his or her team.

Starting at the top

Jethro was the father-in-law of Moses in the Bible. He should be regarded as the patron saint of all management consultants! He certainly gave Moses some good advice, after the exodus of the twelve tribes of Israel from Egypt, on the need for an accountable structure. One day, while the tribes of Israel were in the desert, he saw Moses sitting with people crowding around him from morning till evening, counselling them and solving disputes.

'This is not the best way to do it,' said Jethro. 'You will only wear yourself out and wear out all the people who are here. The task is too heavy for you; you cannot do it by yourself. Now listen to me . . .'

Jethro told Moses that he must get his priorities right and put the work that only he could do – his role as prophet – first. How could he make time to do that?

'You must yourself search for capable, God-fearing men among all the people; honest and incorruptible men,' Jethro told him. 'Then appoint them as leaders of the people – over units of a thousand, of a hundred, of fifty and ten. They shall sit as a permanent court for the people; they must refer difficult cases to you but decide simple cases themselves. In this way your burden will be lightened, and they will share it with you. If you do this, God will give you strength, and you will be able to go on. And, moreover, this whole people will here and now regain peace and harmony.'

Moses was a leader with humility, which always include being open to criticism and constructive suggestions. We are told that he did all that Jethro asked of him.

There is a tendency higher up in an organization to have too few people reporting to the next level. People who work in the middle levels of an organization become aware that one of the reasons they do not give of their best is that the person above them is often doing their job for them. This is partly due to the fact that each level does not have enough people reporting to it. (You may have noticed in the box above that Jethro divided the hundred into two groups of fifty, so that the leader in charge there had only two leaders reporting to him – not enough. I like to think that this is why eventually 'Moses sent his father-in-law on his way, and he went back to his own country.')

If you have only two people reporting to you, it is perfectly possible, if you work hard, to do their jobs for them. But if you have seven or eight people reporting to you, the structure is encouraging you to delegate or collapse. As a rule of thumb, aim to build a structure of working groups composed of between five and fifteen people. Such a policy will insure you against the common mistake of building into the structure too many levels of leadership or management. As Albert Einstein said, 'Everything should be made as simple as possible but not simpler.'

The organizational structure is the bony skeleton of the organization. It should be functional in terms of the purpose, so that it adequately supports the muscle power and a robust communication system. Simplicity must be a hallmark at every level. Finally, it will work only if its cells and organs are free and flexible enough to be realigned at short notice to meet the challenges of a rapidly changing environment.

It is important always to keep coming back to *purpose* (see Chapter 6). A hospital exists to make sick people better, whatever ends are pursued by some of the staff working there. There is always a truth about why organizations are there – or what they should be doing – but it is often a great intellectual struggle to achieve and maintain clarity on the matter. This is especially true in a rapidly changing social, technological and economic situation. Changes in the methods or means by which the purposes are achieved are then demanded. Sometimes they call into question the fundamental purpose of the organization.

It follows that if you are unable to define the purpose or to formulate any vision for the organization, you will not be able to appraise its present structure or embark upon any meaningful organizational development. It often requires considerable courage, decisiveness and determination to set about reorganizing to achieve the purpose more effectively in the present and in the future. Organizations tend to resist change. They like to live in the past, usually the recent past. The need for group cohesiveness – to remain together just as we are – is a powerful one. It can work against the leader as well as for him or her. No organization can handle too much change all at once. The leader as chief executive needs a political sense to bring about the necessary changes with the minimum disruption, but if you do not tackle the agenda you are no leader.

A GOOD LEADER DELEGATES

From the story of Moses on pages 161–162, it is clear that delegating and organizing are closely related. Jethro advised Moses to delegate and that meant setting up an organization. To delegate means to give a subordinate the authority and freedom to handle certain matters on his or her own initiative, with the confidence that they can do the job successfully. It is not to be confused with abdication.

<table>
<tr><td>Delegation</td><td>Telling a subordinate the results required and giving them the authority – 'Do it your way and ask for help if required.'</td></tr>
<tr><td>Abdication</td><td>Relinquishing responsibility for the job – 'Do it any way you like but don't ask for help if it goes wrong.'</td></tr>
</table>

Sometimes people assume that an individual (or an organization) can delegate more at will. But delegation can only happen effectively if, for example, the right staff have been selected and trained for the job. For delegation to happen an organization needs to pursue definite policies over selection, training, appraising performance and career planning.

Remember that you should not delegate unless you are willing to give the person concerned the necessary authority to do the job, matched with your supportive trust in him or her. Be available to discuss progress or to help with any problems the subordinate cannot deal with themselves. Grip your desk hard and do not interfere! Accept the fact that the job will be done differently from the way that you would have done it, but will still fall within the bounds of success. Such effective delegation serves a twofold purpose: it frees you for constructive work on larger projects, and it is a necessary technique for furthering the growth and development of subordinates. Make sure that the person knows what results are expected of them and make them accountable for their performance.

RESTRUCTURING INDIVIDUAL JOBS

A possible object for your organizing ability or skill is the jobs that individuals are doing. Are they unnecessarily boring, dull or monotonous? It is vital to consult the person concerned here, because the profile of individual needs is as unique as a set of fingerprints. What seems repetitive to you may be reassuringly safe to someone else. Aptitude varies widely, and an apparently boring and mundane job may seem interesting and responsible to the particular individual who is doing it. To you and me, a hundred sheep all look the same but to the good shepherd they are all individuals.

ORGANIZING YOURSELF

Sure signs of whether or not you are capable of executing the function of organizing lie in your own life. A good indicator is whether or not you are good at organizing your own time. It is essential for the leader to make time to think, both about the present and the future. That means in the first place an awareness of the value of time and the economical use of it. 'Ask me for anything', Napoleon used to say, 'except for time.' He knew that he had only twenty-four hours a day like anyone else, but he used time more effectively.

One method of developing your awareness and skill in time management is to keep a detailed diary of how you are spending your time. Often this reveals that relatively little time is being given to the key activities of leadership and communication, let alone thinking about decisions or problems. People dropping in during the morning, chatting or drinking coffee, or indiscriminate attention to all your emails at they come in can take up half your time. At the end of the day you go home with that uncomfortable feeling that you have not really achieved anything.

Making time to think

What advice can be offered to a leader? He must discipline himself and lead a carefully regulated and ordered life. He must allow a certain amount of time for quiet thought and reflection; the best times are in the early morning, and in the evening. The quality, good or bad, of any action which is to be taken will vary directly with the time spent in thinking; against this, he must not be rigid; his decisions and plans must be readily adaptable to changing situations. A certain ruthlessness is essential, particularly with inefficiency and also with those who would waste his time. People will accept this, provided the leader is ruthless with himself . . .

Most leaders will find there is so much to do and so little time to do it; that was my experience in the military sphere. My answer to that is not to worry; what is needed is a quiet contemplation of all aspects of the problem, followed by a decision – and it is fatal to worry afterwards.

Field Marshal Viscount Montgomery

Here are some practical suggestions drawn from my book *Effective Time Management* (Pan Macmillan, 2009) to help you to make the best use of your time at work. Check yourself against this ten-point programme once a month for the next six months.

1. **Develop a personal sense of time**
   Do not rely on memory or assume that you know where your time goes. For one or two weeks keep a record. Become more aware of the value of your time and resolve to use it well.

2. **Identify your longer-term goals and policies**
   The clearer you are about your longer-term ends the easier you will find it to identify your priorities. Policies are decisions about principles: they help you to make many daily decisions without having to waste too much time on them.

3. **Make middle-term plans**
   You should be able to translate fluently *purpose* into *aims*, and *aims* into *objectives* (see pages 80–81) Plan your work on aims and objectives in terms of opportunities and desired results, priorities and deadlines.

4. Plan the day

Make a list of what you want to do each day. Arrange it or mark it in some order of priority. Learn to say no, otherwise you will become merely a slave to the priorities of others.

5. Make best use of your best time

Your best time is when you do your best work. Where possible, always use it for important tasks. Have some planned quiet periods for creative thinking.

6. Organize your administrative work

Work out systems for handling paperwork, dealing with emails and making telephone calls, so that you do not fragment your day. Make administration your servant and not your master.

7. Manage meetings

Work out the agenda carefully, allotting time for each item. Start on time and end on time. Use your skills as a leader to make meetings both businesslike and enjoyable.

8. Delegate effectively

Where possible, delegate as much administrative responsibility as you can. The reason for doing so is to free yourself for exercising the kind of leadership that your position requires.

9. Make use of committed time

Committed time is time given over to specific purposes, such as travel. Use waiting time or travelling time to think, plan, read or make calls.

10. Manage your health

Time management is primarily about the *quality* of your time, not about its *quantity*. Follow common-sense guidelines over sleep, diet, exercise and holidays.

Achieve a balance between work and private life that works for you and keeps you free from the toxic kinds of stress.

SUMMARY

Organizing is the function of arranging parts into a working order. 'Structure is a means for attaining the objectives and goals of an institution,' writes Peter Drucker. This is no more than another application of the Three Circles model.

At *group level* you may have to organize for results by setting up **subgroups**. At *organization level*, however, the principle may mean introducing **structural changes** to respond to changes in the task, technology or the environment. This chapter contains a guide for carrying out a survey of your own organization, based upon common-sense principles. Bringing about the changes will, of course, require considerable powers of leadership.

To be effective as a leader you should be able to organize your own work. You should become especially good at managing your time, for it is your most precious resource. 'Time wasted is existence, used is life,' wrote the poet Edward Young. So it is worth recalling to yourself often that nothing belongs to you but your time, and you have it even if you have nothing else.

> *It is not enough to be busy. The question is:*
> *What are you busy about?*
>   Henry Thoreau

CHECKLIST:
ORGANIZING

Organizing is an important function in meeting all three areas of the Three Circles model. Check your organizing ability in the following areas.

	Yes	No

GROUP

	Yes	No
Is the size of the working group correct and are the right people working together?	☐	☐
Is there a need for subgroups to be constituted?	☐	☐
Are there regular opportunities or procedures for genuine consultation with the group before taking decisions affecting them, e.g. decisions relating to work plans and output, work methods and standards, work measurement and overtime working?	☐	☐

ORGANIZATION

	Yes	No
Are you clear on the purpose of the organization and how the various parts of it work together to achieve that end?	☐	☐
Is there an effective system for staffing the organization and training? Is there a fair dismissal procedure?	☐	☐
Do you carry out regular surveys of the organization to check:		
the size of all working groups?	☐	☐
the number of leadership levels?	☐	☐
the growth of unnecessary complexity?	☐	☐
line and staff cooperation?	☐	☐
that the communication systems are working properly?	☐	☐

YOURSELF

Are there ways in which you could organize your personal and working life, e.g. how your deal with your personal administration, in order to be a more effective leader? ☐ ☐

Do you delegate sufficiently? ☐ ☐

Can you identify at least three steps you can take in order to become a better organizer of your time? ☐ ☐

1. ....

2. ....

3. ....

13

SETTING AN EXAMPLE

'The lantern carrier should go ahead.'
Japanese proverb

As a leader you cannot help setting an example – the question is whether it will be a good or a bad one. If you are setting a good example people will tend not to be too aware of it, but they will certainly notice and comment upon a bad example. The Russians have a saying, 'Nothing is so contagious as a bad example.' This is something long remarked upon by wise men. Francis Bacon said: 'He that gives good advice builds with one hand. He that gives good counsel and example builds with both. But he that gives good admonition and bad example builds with one hand and pulls down with the other.'

Example is important because people take in information more through their eyes than their ears. What they see you do is far more powerful than what they hear you say. The basic principle is that your word and example should always go together – they should support each other. If they conflict, you must expect people to follow your example and not your precept. 'Don't do as I do, do as I say' – those words should never pass the lips of a true leader, except in so far as they acknowledge that he or she is aspiring towards a common high standard and, being human, is all too aware of his or her own shortcomings. People will respect you if you try to set the right example, even if you fall short on occasion.

IN THE TASK AREA

A root meaning of 'leadership' is leading in the sense of literally going out in front of others. An Alpine guide, for example, is doing this in using his or her own body to convey to the followers in what direction they should be travelling. When we widen the reference to non-physical situations, the leader is still the person who gives others a sense of direction in a given field by their own behaviour. Leadership implies the personal willingness to go out in front – accepting the risks involved – in order to ensure that your team goes in the right direction and at the right speed.

To continue the analogy, if you are too far ahead of the group – too advanced in your thinking – you run the risk of losing contact with them altogether. If you are too far behind, however, you may find yourself saying, like a politician in the French Revolution of 1848 who was trying to force his way through a mob of which he was one of the chief instigators, 'Let me pass, I have to follow them, I am their leader.'

Just how much of an example you should set by personally doing the work yourself depends upon your level of leadership. At the lower levels you should expect to lead by doing the job yourself – or part of it at least – in the way you expect it to be done. But the other functions of leadership, notably controlling and coordinating, should take priority if there is any conflict over how your time should be spent.

In the military field this aspect of leadership tends to be

crystal clear. The platoon commander is expected to lead his platoon from the front; the squadron leader flies his own fighter as well as controlling the squadron. At a certain level, however, the military commander does not lead the attack in person. 'We shall be right behind you on the day, sir,' said one eager sergeant to General Slim in Burma in the Second World War. 'Make no mistake, Sergeant.' replied Slim with a smile, 'when the day comes you will be several miles in front of me!'

Does the senior leader then stop leading by example? Not necessarily. The fact that he or she at some stage in their career has led 'from the front' in the basic task is itself an important factor in winning the respect of their younger colleagues at all levels. It has the added practical advantage that people know such a leader will not ask them to do what they would not be willing to do themselves – or to have done in the past. If the leader is not willing to do the job themselves they can hardly command others to do it.

Ask not of others . . .

At the age of twenty-one I was working as a deckhand on a Hull fishing trawler. The mate in charge of the deckhands was a large bully of a man with a chip on his shoulder, for he had recently been a skipper but lost his ticket through incompetence.

One afternoon, in a winter storm near Iceland, he told one of the men to shin up the mast and adjust an unsafe navigation light. 'Not bloody likely,' said the man, looking at the kicking mast and hissing waves. 'You do it, Bill,' thundered the mate to another deckhand. 'Not me,' replied Bill with a shrug. The mate began to shout and swear at us all.

Attracted by the commotion on deck, the skipper came down from the bridge. 'What's up?' he asked. The mate told him. 'Why don't you go up yourself?' the skipper said to the mate, looking him in the eye. Silence. 'Right, I'll do it myself,' said the skipper, and began to pull off his oilskin. He meant it too. At once three or four men stepped forward and volunteered, for we had no desire to lose our navigator overboard.

Which was the true leader – the mate or the skipper?

Even at the more senior levels of leadership it is sometimes possible for the leader to give what might be called a symbolic example. When Napoleon found a sentry asleep one night he took up the man's musket and stood guard himself for a few hours. Occasionally a senior leader can 'lend a hand', working beside his or her people for an hour or two. Such gestures can have an electric effect upon subordinates, in direct proportion to the rank or seniority of the leader concerned. The grapevine, which can be a positive as well as a negative factor in large organizations, will carry the good news around. When Julius Caesar, their Commander-in-Chief, sat around a mess table with ten soldiers of a Roman legion sharing their meal of bread, meat and rough wine and then in the afternoon took part in their military exercises, the whole Roman Army had heard about it within a few weeks.

Leadership involves the ability to inspire, and people are touched by such imaginative gestures. A gram of example is worth a kilogram of exhortation. Sometimes such a symbolic act can serve to remind a group or an organization of the basic meaning of leadership. It is as if the leader is saying, 'I should like to be with you all more often, especially when there is a dirty or arduous job to be done, but my other responsibilities just do not allow me too. At least what I have done this afternoon is a token that I mean what I say.'

IN THE TEAM AND INDIVIDUAL AREAS

The importance of setting an example in establishing, maintaining, or altering group standards cannot be overstated. Whatever you require the group to do, you should be prepared to do yourself. Punctuality is an obvious instance. If you want each member of the group to help the others with their work, you can best convey that by doing it yourself. The norms of human relations – listening, respecting, communicating and caring – can all be best conveyed by example.

When Jesus wanted to impress upon his disciples that as leaders they should be prepared to meet the needs of individuals, he did not give them a long lecture on social psychology. Instead he took a bowl, a jug of water and a towel, knelt down and washed their dusty feet. By thus performing the functions of a lowly household servant he was also teaching them the need for humility as leaders – a virtue in stark contrast to the domineering arrogance of many of the kings of the day.

'It is certain,' wrote Shakespeare in *King Henry IV*, 'that either wise bearing or ignorant carriage is caught, as men take diseases, therefore let men take heed of their company.' Example is contagious. It is action or conduct which induces imitation. Children are naturally imitative: it is the way they learn. As adults we retain that characteristic. In creating the right climate of purpose, unity and teamwork, how you bear yourself as leader can be decisive.

'You mention integrity as an important quality,' a manager asked Lord Slim at a large conference for managers and directors. 'Can you suggest how this quality can be spread in industry?' 'Yes, by example,' replied Slim.

Good example, then, has creative power, especially if it

involves an element of self-sacrifice. It can work in people's minds to alter their ways. That process may take time, but the leader whose example backs up his words puts himself in an unassailable position. No one can accuse him of hypocrisy; of preaching one thing and doing another.

That is what gave Nelson Mandela his unique moral authority as a leader – he shared the dangers, hardships and sufferings of his people. Long years of imprisonment on Robben Island may have removed him from the land of South Africa, but it enhanced his stature as a leader by example. It gave him greater power to inspire others – even some of his captors.

You can see now that the principle of leading by example is a challenging one, for it involves not only what you *do* but also who you *are* and how you choose to live. It reminds you that leadership can never be a thing apart from the rest of your life. In practical terms your own example is the most powerful weapon at your command. As Dag Hammarskjold, Secretary General of the United Nations until 1961, wrote to himself one night in his diary: 'Your position never gives you the right to command. It only imposes on you the duty of so living your life that others can receive your orders without being humiliated.' Not long after he wrote those words Hammarskjold lost his life when the aircraft he was in crashed. He was on his way to try to bring peace to a troubled area in central Africa.

SUMMARY

'Leadership *is* example,' wrote one officer cadet on his observation sheet after a two-week exercise while I was at Sandhurst. I have often reflected on his words. It seems to me that true leaders are linked by this principle, that in some way or other they set an example – **they *do* or *live* what they preach or require in others**. This separates them from the mere talkers. They lead from the front. They share in the fortunes of their people, not claiming any special privileges or exemptions. They are among their people, not over them – servants rather than masters.

Example is relevant to the *task* circle, as the original meaning of leadership – going out in front – makes clear. You lead only where you are willing to go yourself. Where that physical leading is not appropriate you can set an example, for instance by working hard or being accurate and well informed. Example can help you to *build the team*, for you can illustrate by example the group standards you are seeking to maintain or alter for the better. The *individual* who knows you or sees you from afar may be inspired to emulate you.

You may need some creative imagination to apply this principle, but apply it you must if you are committed to becoming a better leader. If it calls for an element of self-denial or sacrifice on your part, so that you share fully in the dangers and hardships of your people, so much the better. That will almost certainly win a response.

Ducere est servire (To lead is to serve)

Motto of Britain's Chartered
Institute of Management

CHECKLIST:
SETTING AN EXAMPLE

Which of these statements would you say most applies to you?

People often comment on the good example you set in   ☐
your work.

You never ask others to do what you are not willing to do yourself. ☐

Sometimes your bad example conflicts with all that we are trying to do here. ☐

You are not really aware of the importance of example and are unable to say what kind of one you are giving. ☐

On what occasion in the last month have you deliberately set out to give a lead by your example?

Did your action have any effect on the group or individual?:

(a) Immediately   Yes ☐   No ☐

(b) Some days later   Yes ☐   No ☐

What specific problems in the team maintenance area might you help to solve by giving a better personal example yourself?

1.

2.

If you are a senior leader or an appraiser of other leaders, have you mentioned to others the importance of example in leadership during the last three months?

                          Yes ☐   No ☐

Using the 'brainstorming' approach, see if you can produce three new – more creative – ways in which you and more senior leaders in the organization might set an example. These should be ways you have not tried before.

1.

2.

3.

Have you ever shared in the dangers, labours or hardships of those who look to you for leadership?

PART THREE

GROWING AS
A LEADER

Contrary to what some people seem to believe, there is no such thing as 'instant leadership'. It is not a collection of 'behaviours' or techniques you can acquire on a course. The eight functions and skills described in Part Two have to be developed over a period of time. They involve what you *are* and what you *know* as well as what you are able to *do*. Therefore you need to grow as a leader in a way which involves your leadership qualities, knowledge and skills. What are the conditions for that long-term growth? They lie partly in **yourself** and partly in the **organization** in which you work. Each of these two aspects is the subject of a section that follows.

When you have finished reading and reflecting upon Part Three, and carefully and thoroughly completed the checklists it contains, you should be able to:

● Appreciate the conditions necessary in any **organization** if those with leadership ability or potential are to be fully developed and used.

- Set down on paper the rough draft of a **leadership self-development programme** covering the next five years.
- Identify at least five short-term **action points** for improving your own leadership.

14

DOES YOUR ORGANIZATION DEVELOP LEADERS?

If you are a chief executive or a member of a board of directors, this section should speak directly to you, for it is your responsibility to develop the leadership the organization needs in the present and future. If you are a director of human recourses or such like, you may find here the basis for the plan you need to make.

If you are not yet at those lofty heights, you should still read this chapter, if only in order to assess how far your organization is shaping up to the challenge of leadership development, for your development only partly depends upon your inherent abilities and willingness to stretch yourself. You also have to be in the right situation at the right time. Just as a plant needs light, food and warmth, so you need certain conditions present in the organization. A famous athletics coach used to say that 'champions are planted in the winter, tended in the spring, and blossom in the summer'. Developing leaders is a similar process.

What, then, are these conditions that you should be seeking to create in your organization so that it becomes a more fruitful source for practical leaders? There are ten such conditions or principles.

1. A STRATEGY FOR LEADERSHIP DEVELOPMENT

Organizations who mean business in this field will need to formulate a strategy for leadership development at board of director level or its equivalent.

After formulating a leadership development strategy the board of directors should ensure that:

- A high proportion of those working for the organization know about it: briefing
- There are regular reviews of progress in implementing it: evaluating
- It is updated as new ideas or developments become available: planning.

What should the elements of that strategy be? What are the principles the strategic thinkers must apply?

2. SELECTION PROCEDURES

All organizations have methods of selecting their future leaders. Interviewing, combined with scrutiny of the written application form, CV and references, are still the main methods employed. These traditional methods are often supplemented by assessment techniques that stem directly from the group approach to leadership testing (see page 66) developed in the Second World War. There is scope for much more experiment along these lines.

All that such selection procedures will do, however, is to identify young people in terms of their natural *potential* for enabling a group to achieve a common task, building or maintaining a team and meeting individual needs. The procedure should encompass some estimate of their personality (including temperament), aptitudes and interests in relation to the working situation: the general nature of the task activity and the environment in which it has to be pursued.

Should psychological tests be used? From the leadership angle, the danger of these is that they can be almost too effective in picking 'round pegs' for 'round holes', whereas this kind of matching ignores the dimension of change and the need for creative people in the organization.

Recently a large conglomerate of firms invited me to take part in their annual conference for personnel managers. During the three days we spent together I was struck by their complacency. They had achieved a certain level in their 'personnel policies' as they called them. Welfare and benefits were good, but they were not interested in developing leadership. They seemed resigned to their faceless committee management. They lacked creative thinkers or creative innovation. Some time earlier I had experienced their selection techniques when I was applying for a job there. Psychologists tested applicants for two whole days. These tests certainly enabled them to choose good company men and women, who would fit into present job specifications and not rock the boat. But I wonder now if in that process they did not screen out *all* the creative people. Hence the seeds of the present problems were sown several decades ago.

It is in fact difficult to predict who will be the 'high flyers' in leadership when the organization is selecting managers from relatively young and inexperienced candidates. Good judges of character may be able to sense by intuition when they interview someone with potential for great leadership. Often they may seem to be someone who does not fit the jobs available, for they will come into their own at a higher level, or perhaps in some situation in the future which the leaders of the organization today have not even thought of. Among the young men and women recruited today will probably be those who will be required to lead the organization in the future, which by definition is largely an unknown territory. Just think for a moment of the changes they will have to cope with – and manage – in the decades before then. Just imagine the kind of leadership that will be needed when they eventually reach the top of your organization in those days.

Selecting those with leadership potential is essential. They may not all be high flyers, but then every organization needs mostly mainstream leaders. The exceptionally gifted will tend to select themselves anyway. To whatever degree, however, that potential ability – functional abilities as well as qualities – must be there. Even the best gardener cannot turn a tulip into a rose only by using good fertilizer.

3. TRAINING FOR LEADERSHIP

In my view it is unfair, if not immoral, to give a person a leadership job without giving him or her some training for leadership. Yet hundreds of organizations do just that. It is unfair on that person, but it is even rougher for those whom he or she is expected to lead.

Michael Jones is a brilliant metallurgist. Working hard in his university laboratory, employing X-ray crystallography techniques, he acquired a wide reputation and published many papers. Then, at the age of fifty, he was appointed head of the Materials and Metallurgy Department at Stirlchester University. The academic staff, technicians and secretaries were soon writhing in discontent. 'He is no leader,' one declared. But who was to blame? As

Michael said, 'I have never had any training in leadership or management. It's too late to teach an old dog new tricks now.'

We should think of education or training for leadership as happening at different stages in a person's career. The foundations should have been laid before a person presents himself or herself for a job involving the management of people – at school, in the family and in tertiary education.

The opportunity for training for leadership in the form of a course based on the Three Circles model or its equivalent should come shortly before or after a person has been given a team leadership role. (By 'shortly' I would suggest not more than six months either way.) There are pros and cons for both options.

Before:

- Gives the person a 'sketch map' and guidelines.
- Reduces the likelihood of serious mistakes.
- But they have no direct experience to relate to functional leadership theory.

After:

- The person will bring leadership experience to the course.
- He or she will have encountered difficulties, so will be very motivated to learn.
- But it may already be too late, at least for this job.

The training course concerned, whether it is based on the Three Circles model or not, should be practical and participative – 'learning through doing'. If it is done on an in-house or in-company basis, the course should be adapted to give it maximum relevance to the needs and character of the organization.

The principle of training for leadership should apply at the more senior levels of **operational** and **strategic** leadership. In *How to Grow Leaders* (Kogan Page, 2005) I have described my innovations in this field. Although the centrality of the generic role of leader remains a constant at all levels, the methods employed on leadership programmes for newly appointed operational and strategic leaders are different: less emphasis on skills training, with more focus on exploring and understanding the principles of leadership in the light of one's experience of leading – and being led.

The main issue now for organizations throughout the world is not whether or not to provide leadership development for their senior managers, for such programmes are now common. The question now concerns *quality*. Too often these global programmes fall short of their aim of developing and inspiring strategic leaders.

4. A CAREER DEVELOPMENT POLICY

One survey of 2,000 chief executives revealed that the average age when they entered senior management was thirty-two. They achieved the top job at an average age of forty-one. On the way up these 'high flyers' had worked in more than eight different jobs in two or three different organizations. Behind these facts we can glimpse an essential story, admittedly speeded up in the case of budding chief executives but true for all who aspire to rise as leaders in organizations. It is the process by which a specialist becomes a generalist by planned career moves.

The chief executive of a bottling company mentioned in our conversation that he had moved his finance director and put him in charge of marketing and distribution. 'He should be challenging for my job soon,' he added. 'He has what it takes, but he lacks experience of the business as a whole. He realizes that, and we have agreed on this move as part of his development.'

The story or process of your career can be represented as being like the shape of an hourglass or egg timer. As you move upward through the narrow neck of the glass you will begin to acquire the wider knowledge or experience of the purpose of the organization as a whole, as compared with your specialized part or contribution within it. That career movement, however, sets up the need for development in leadership, communication and decision making where you are not the technical expert.

Strategic Leadership
Decision making
Creative thinking
Communication

Narrow neck of specialization

General Education

From specialist to business leader

Much has been spoken about the 'small is beautiful' concept in organizations. From the human angle there is indeed much to be said for working in small organizations or companies. Communication, for example, tends to be less of a problem, but the potential advantages of size are not only economic ones. They include the ability to offer people the opportunity of developing and training experience in other divisions or companies within the group. Strangely enough, many very large organizations do not capitalize on this asset. They may move people within functions, such as finance, but they do not really cross-post them. Why, then, you may ask, have a large organization?

If your organization is getting it right it will not allow the leaders of tomorrow to stagnate in jobs. That does not mean they should be moved every year before their mistakes have a chance to catch up on them! There has to be time to achieve some objectives, to build up a track record, but the emphasis should be upon onwards and upwards. That means wider knowledge, gained through working in a range of functional areas, on the staff as well as in line management. It may include secondments and periods away from the organization altogether. This situational approach, however, should be coupled with a broadening and deepening of the manager's study of universal leadership. Without raising false expectations it is always appropriate to explain to the person concerned precisely *why* the move is being proposed. Otherwise an appointment to manage your big plant in Siberia may look more like a punishment than an opportunity!

5. LINE MANAGERS AS LEADERSHIP MENTORS

If line managers are taking the Three Circles approach seriously they will accept that developing the individual includes developing their leadership potential. That involves far more than just sending the person concerned on an appropriate training course. It means trying to do 'on the job' leadership training. That involves the function of evaluating in the form of appraising the individual – identifying strengths and weaknesses, encouraging, advising and listening. An annual formal appraisal interview should be no more than a safety net, a ratification of points discussed. If so, it need not last more than ten minutes.

Before and after a person goes on a leadership course he or she should be briefed and debriefed by the person they report to. The first talk is to establish clearly why the organization thinks it worth spending their money and the individual's time on the course. The person's training needs and the course objectives have to tie up. After the course is over, the line manager should want to listen to the individual's action points so that help, support and encouragement can be given in the period of implementation. This may entail changes in the way the department or division is organized or run, which will need digesting – sometimes over a drink.

If your line managers are themselves leaders of some stature, leading by example as well as precept, the young managers will be learning a great deal more from working with them, observing them and talking to them than they can ever put into words. As one chief executive said to me, talking of his own early mentor, 'At a crisis in my youth, he taught me the wisdom of choice – to try and fail is at least to learn; to fail to try is to suffer the inestimable loss of what might have been.'

To find such a mentor for a young leader is of immeasurable value. If an organization can promote respect and affection among its managers, then they will be far more likely to help each other to grow as effective leaders. We are all learners in this school.

6. RESEARCH AND DEVELOPMENT

As in any other field, there is a certain amount of technical expertise involved in developing leadership. The textbooks tend to be written in jargon. You need to have been around for a certain time within that sphere before you can catch up with what is happening. Therefore, an organization of any size needs to have its specialist in leadership research and development, or at least access to one. That specialist should always be associated with a small group of line managers or their equivalents who have a more-than-average interest in the subject and who can be realistic.

Apart from looking at new ideas, courses and training aids, such specialists might also be charged with evaluating the effectiveness of courses, training the trainers (who may be line managers) and advising the top management on the progress of their strategy. You will recall that *evaluating* is a major generic leadership function, but alas it is seldom applied with any rigour to corporate or collegiate leadership development programmes by those who lead them. It is a case of 'Physician, heal thyself'.

7. GETTING THE STRUCTURES RIGHT

Nothing causes more frustration or impedes leadership development more than a poor organizational structure. As chief executive a key part of your leadership – the organizing function at your level – must be devoted to getting the structure right. It will never be perfectly right, but some organizations are definitely worse than others in this respect. Often you will be faced with an option of difficulties.

The Kindermere Healthcare Trust has grown in the last five years to thirty-two private hospitals, scattered throughout the United Kingdom. It now has 3,000 employees. There are thirty-two matrons, all reporting to one Chief Nursing Officer in London. Should KHT *regionalise* in order to create a smaller span of control? But to do so means introducing *another level of management*. What would you do?

What matters in organizational design is that it should be possible for the leaders to lead. That means that they should have the time to talk to their teams and not be sentenced to solitary confinement behind a desk.

Organizational structure alone does not guarantee good leadership, but if it gets very out of date, top heavy or lopsided, it can make the work of leadership extremely difficult. Sometimes an organization will then fall into a vicious circle. Conservative managers or leaders may maintain time-honoured structures despite the fact that they have become rigid or dysfunctional. Those structures in turn attract or develop managers who cannot lead, and so it goes on. The remedy is to get the structure right and keep it in trim.

8. SELF-DEVELOPMENT

Throughout this book I have assumed that you 'own' the problem of how to develop *your* leadership potential, so that it becomes real, effective and rewarding. The following chapter is entirely on that theme, but I believe that the organization should already have empowered you to develop your leadership potential, long before you picked up this book.

The benefit for an organization in applying this principle is that it can enter into a *partnership* with its young leaders or leaders-to-be which is to their mutual advantage. The organization can supply opportunities, training and encouragement, whereas the budding leaders bring high motivation and the willingness to learn. Both have to be honest with each other in their relationship. In particular the organization must strive to give its honest impressions, in the form of realistic feedback, of how far up the ladder of promotion a person is likely to rise. Has he or she the makings of a senior-level leader? Those impressions may prove wrong, but they should be given.

The apparent disadvantage of such a policy, of course, is that the manager concerned may come to place his or her self-development as a leader in front of the needs of the organization, but this drawback does not stand up to serious examination. Both the organization and the individual concerned may agree that the right next opportunity is lacking, and so it makes sense to look elsewhere. Remember those 2,000 chief executives on page 188? On average they had worked for *two or more* organizations.

A good organization will probably produce more leaders than it can use at senior level, for all pyramids narrow towards the top. 'Why should we train leaders for other companies?' one manager once asked me. Yet most organizations import leaders at one level or another and at certain times, and so they should be willing to export them as well. Besides, it is surely no bad thing to improve the whole industry or field of work that you are active in by training some of its leaders. Those who give freely usually find that sooner or later they also receive in equal measure.

9. ORGANIZATIONAL CULTURE

The prevailing temper of a group or organization is another important factor in developing leadership. Using an analogy of the weather, it is plain what Montgomery meant by the 'atmosphere' in an organization (page 105). That kind of 'weather' is largely an invasion by the situation, or at least as people perceive it. When chill winds blow in the environment an organization can catch a cold; it may even die of pneumonia. But organizational climate implies a longer-term ethos: the prevailing atmosphere generated *within* the organization. In this sense we might imagine an organization as a large market-garden greenhouse. To some extent the people working inside can create their own climate. In such a building there are many dials upon which the elements of climate, such as temperature and humidity, can be read, and so it is with organizations. We want a warm, friendly atmosphere. That usually brings out the best in people, but it should not be too cosy. To change the analogy, it is no good if the crew are sitting down below drinking coffee and being friendly with each other if the ship is driving towards the rocks.

Clearly, much of the ethos of an organization will be set by its leaders. They need to articulate from time to time its guiding beliefs or values. It is they who will set an example of cheerfulness at all times, for difficult tasks do not preclude enjoyment and fun. They can demonstrate by example the importance of caring for individuals if they want those individuals to care for the common enterprise in return. I believe there are there distinctive elements in the character or tone of some organizations which encourage the spread of leadership at all levels. For outcomes of conditions that might be found in an organizational climate, see the table overleaf.

LEADERSHIP DEVELOPMENT FACTORS IN THE ORGANIZATIONAL CLIMATE

CONDITIONS	NOTES
Centrifugal	Authority/power constantly tends to move *from* the centre (as opposed to a centripetal organization, where it goes *to* the centre). Plenty of delegation is one symptom. Responsibility flows outwards.
Tolerance of mistakes	Without mistakes there is no progress. There is a policy of trust and confidence in people, backed by training.
Forward-looking	Despite past achievements a proud organization is oriented towards the future. It thinks in terms of purpose, aims and objectives.
Teamwork	The emphasis falls upon working in teams and as one big team. Teams imply good leaders. Therefore these will be naturally encouraged to emerge.
More equity	Where most outward status distinctions are being progressively abandoned, people are perceived to be equal in value. Then leadership becomes that much more important for getting things done.

The climate or ethos of an organization is primarily the responsibility of the senior leadership, for it cannot be divorced from the overall effectiveness of the organization in terms of achieving the common task, working as a team and developing individuals. Developing the leadership potential in individuals is a special instance of the third circle of the Three Circles model. Does the climate of your organization hatch out leadership, or does it stifle it? You may recall the Indian proverb that nothing grows under the great banyan tree.

10. THE CHIEF EXECUTIVE

'As the chief man or woman of a city is, so will be the people,' observed the author of the Book of Ecclesiastes in the Bible. So much depends upon the top leader, not least in terms of forming and implementing a strategy for developing leadership in the organization.

The degree of leadership present in the chief executive soon becomes apparent when it comes to talking about the development of leadership within his or her organization. There are often three broad types of response.

- 'Leadership is just what my managers need. Yes, go ahead and train them. Oh no, we don't need it in the boardroom – we're far too busy for that sort of thing.'

- 'I see what you mean. But I am too old or set in my ways to change my ways, and that goes for my senior colleagues too. Yet we will give you all the support and backing we can. When are you running the first programme? I'll come along.'

- 'Leadership development? We are the ones who need it first. I'll invite my senior colleagues to the first seminar. Then we shall take it from there. I see it very much as part of our strategy for this company over the next five years.'

Even if the chief executive is committed – and leading by example – he or she still has to persuade the senior leadership group to make the journey as well. That can be a formidable task. Most top management teams do not appreciate what such a policy implies, and certainly not what a total commitment to it entails. But then it is the first duty of the chief executive to be a team leader of his or her senior operational leaders – the organization's key steering group.

SUMMARY

Few organizations are really geared towards developing to the full the *leadership potential* within them. Sometimes this may be due to the fact that they place little or no premium upon it, assuming either that it is not important or that the conventional management training will provide it. Only the best organizations show real and sustained commitment to selecting and developing their business leaders. Why? *Because those organizations know from experience that effective leadership at all levels is essential for their continued success.*

The principles which determined organizations should apply are the same, but of course the ways in which they are applied will differ according to circumstances. Those principles are as follows.

- Formulate a policy for leadership development at the highest level.
- Place a priority on leadership potential in selection procedures.
- Train leaders on properly designed courses.
- Plan careers so as to give appropriate experience.
- Turn all line managers into leadership mentors or coaches 'on the job'.
- Build a specialist resource in this area.
- Evolve an organizational structure that favours the exercise of leadership.
- Encourage all leaders to 'own' their own self-development.

- Secure a climate or ethos which supports good leadership.
- Give a positive lead from the top – lead by example.

To learn is a natural pleasure, not confined to philosophers but common to all men.

Aristotle

CHECKLIST:
DOES YOUR ORGANIZATION DEVELOP LEADERS?

	Yes	No
Do you have a clear strategy for building good human relations which includes developing leadership at every level?	☐	☐
When selecting people for management jobs, do you assess them in terms of their functional leadership abilities (task, team and individual) and the associated qualities of personality and character?	☐	☐

Are appointed team leaders given a minimum of two days of leadership training?

Always ☐   Sometimes ☐   Never ☐

	Yes	No
Do you have some system for career development so that future senior leaders broaden their experience and knowledge?	☐	☐
Are all line managers convinced that they are the real leadership trainers, however effective they are in that role?	☐	☐
Is there a specialist 'research and development' team that is keeping the organization and its line managers up to date – and up to the mark?	☐	☐
Has your organizational structure been evolved with good leadership in mind?	☐	☐
Do leaders, actual or potential, realize that they are the ones who 'own' their self-development?	☐	☐

Would you say that there was room for improving the organizational culture or ethos?

A great deal ☐   Some ☐   None ☐

Are your top leaders really behind leadership development?

Whole-heartedly ☐   Half-heartedly ☐   Not yet ☐

15

YOUR LEADERSHIP SELF-DEVELOPMENT PROGRAMME

'Look well into yourself; there is a source which will always spring up if you will search there.'
Marcus Aurelius

Leadership courses usually end with a session on **action points.** We have now reached this point in our journey together. So, in your own individual course in leadership you should be drawing together the various action points you have been writing down. They should form the basis for your leadership self-development programme. As all forward thinking should be done in terms of priorities, it may be helpful to divide your plan into:

- short term: points you can implement immediately, or within the next year
- middle term: actions or developments that may take up to three years to complete
- long term: states or stages you would like to achieve by some date in the four- to ten-year range.

Behind this approach lies the basic assumption of this book, namely, that you are the person who is primarily responsible for your own leadership development. Unless there is some leadership in you in the first place this book will not have spoken to you anyway. For, like Albert Schweitzer, 'I do not believe that we can put into anyone ideas which are not in him anyway. As a rule there are in everyone some good ideas, like tinder. But much of this tinder catches fire only when it meets some flame or spark from outside; that is, from some other person.'

In tending that fire you can at best hope for a high degree of partnership with the organization you happen to be working in at present. You have to see whether it can come up with the right opportunities at the right time, for it can be frustrating to have leadership ability and not to be able to use it. You can teach a child about the theory and principles of riding a bicycle, but there comes a day when you have to give them a bicycle to ride.

The key question is, of course, are you the right person for that job from the organization's point of view as well as your own? Does your self-perception match up with the perceptions that others are forming of you? Are you ready for that opportunity?

Experience in successively more challenging or broader leadership positions is essential for those who are destined for senior leadership jobs. It should not be protracted. As Thomas Hardy said, 'experience is as to intensity and not duration'. But experience by itself, as we have seen, is only one pillar of learning. The other constitutes that growing body of theory, principles, ideas, examples, skills and techniques – your personal and practical leadership philosophy. One possible action point is to keep a notebook for further quotations, examples or ideas relevant to leadership as you come across them. You may also like to keep a file for articles or newspaper cuttings.

To repeat the point, in a very real sense leadership cannot

be taught; it can only be learned. If you work hard at it – given a modicum of potential – you will improve. Indeed, someone of modest natural ability who works hard at the task, team and individual circles will eventually outstrip a person of high natural ability who is lazy and instinctive about it, for the latter's faults will grow bigger like weeds over the years. He or she will not be able to transfer their learnings from one situation to another because they never understood the principles of why they were successful.

OBSERVE CAREFULLY

This leads me to emphasize again one important way of improving your leadership in a fairly painless way – by observation. From our childhood at home and schooldays onwards we are all observing leaders. At work we have first-hand experience of leadership at the receiving end. Alas, we so often forget in later life to do and be what we so wanted our first manager to do and be.

Exercise 8: Learning from observation
Take a piece of paper and a pen. List three leaders that you have worked with whom you would rate as good, adequate and weak. Now identify the positive and negative lessons you learned from them.

It is often easier to learn more about leadership from a bad leader than from a good one – 'knowledge of good bought dear by knowing ill', as Shakespeare put it. Good leadership is often so silent, so self-effacing that you are hardly aware of it, but bad leadership always shouts at you. You will see lack of awareness or understanding, insensitivity, want of firmness, missing functions, integrity over-compromised and a host of other shortcomings. Try to be objective, like a scientist, and observe the effects on the group and yourself in the three key areas of task, team and individual. You may also have noticed that, as a chief executive once commented to me, 'there is almost no extreme of poor performance which cannot be reached by a person or a group of people given sufficient lack of encouragement'. Do you agree?

If you are fortunate you will work with leaders who exemplify some, if not all, of the principles in this book. If you are still more fortunate your leader will also be a mentor; a teacher. We get that word from an actual man named Mentor, the friend to whom Odysseus entrusted the education of his son Telemachus when he went off to the Trojan War. His name now signifies a wise counsellor or guide. Behind many managers in their early careers there are such mentors.

Andrew Carnegie, a great American industrialist of the nineteenth century, owed much to his senior, Thomas A. Scott. As head of the Western Division of the Pennsylvania Railroad, Scott recognized talent and the desire to learn in the young telegrapher assigned to him.

By giving Carnegie increasing responsibility and by providing him with the opportunity to learn through close personal observation, Scott added to Carnegie's self-confidence and sense of achievement. Because of his own personal strength and achievement, Scott did not fear Carnegie's strong personality and drive. Rather, he gave it full play in encouraging Carnegie to use his initiative and to aim high.

In his mellow years Carnegie gave his vast fortune away, and among other things founded 3,000 public libraries in the United Kingdom, his original homeland. 'The man who dies rich dies disgraced,' he wrote, and he was true to his own philosophy.

RECOGNIZE OPPORTUNITIES

You could say that Carnegie was lucky to have such a boss as Scott. Luck, in the sense of events or circumstances which seem to work for you or against you, does certainly play a part in the career of any leader. If General Gott had not been killed in a plane crash, for instance, Montgomery would not have taken over the Eighth Army. You would be foolish if you did not recognize the hand of luck. It is an uncomfortable factor to live with, but it is undeniably there in every sphere of life.

If you are going to be effective as a leader, however, you need to adopt a positive policy towards luck. The worst policy you can adopt is to rely upon luck, except in extreme circumstances where there is literally nothing else you can do. For to some extent you can make your own luck. 'A wise man will make more opportunities than he finds,' said Bacon.

Whether the opportunities come within your present organization or elsewhere in your chosen field, you will be an unlucky person indeed if none come your way. If you set yourself firmly upon the path of leadership you will begin to see such opportunities. You may be given them out of the blue, or you may have to reach out and get them.

On being prepared

Occasionally, I have heard some young man say cynically that advancement is usually the result of 'getting the lucky breaks'. This is a defeatist attitude that I deplore. It would be less than honest to say that good fortune – being there, in the right place, when the lightning strikes – does not play its part. Yet when opportunity comes, even by chance, the man must be prepared, must be able to deliver; otherwise, his triumph will be short-lived. A steady rise to a position of pre-eminence most often comes with hard work, constant effort at self-improvement – and devotion to principle.

One day during my White House years, I called in an assistant – a highly competent man of fine personality – and asked him if he would like to have a more responsible and remunerative job which was then open. I explained that he would be operating rather independently, largely responsible for his own decisions. He thought a moment and then said, 'No, I'd be no good at it. I am a No. 2 man – and I think a good one – but I am not a No. 1 man. I am not fitted for such a job, and I don't want it'.

Although his answer startled me, I respected his honesty. Moreover, this world always needs competent No. 2 men, also good No. 3, No. 4 and No. 5 men – and each, on his own level, can be a good performer.

Yet I would urge any young man or woman with ambition never to be too hasty in concluding that he or she doesn't have the stature for top leadership. Often I have seen a man who had doubts about his own resources rise to the occasion and perform with great competence when the opportunity finally came.

Dwight D. Eisenhower

The more that you examine life, the less the part that chance or luck seems to play in the world of your work, if you are brutally honest with yourself. A woman spectator called out to a famous golfer during a tournament, 'Hey, that was a lucky shot!' The golfer turned round and said, 'Lady, the more I practise the luckier I get!'

If you work hard at your trade – in this case leadership – you will attract opportunities like a magnet. The skill is in observing to the full, in every department of the art of leadership, the motto *Be prepared*. When they congratulated

Louis Pasteur on his discovery, apparently by accident, of the process of pasteurization, he replied, 'Chance favours only the prepared mind.' The secret therefore is to work hard at leadership today, and tomorrow will largely take care of itself. Seize the small opportunities, and the big ones will find their way to you.

How you will react in a very senior leadership position will not be known until you get there. You may drag it down to your own level of incompetence, or you may grow into the job. The way you actually perform in that position will depend largely upon your self-development. As that progresses you may want to revise your preliminary estimate of how high a leadership mountain you can climb.

FIND YOUR MOTIVATION

Whether or not you are prepared to devote what Pasteur called 'patient studies and persevering efforts' to developing your leadership potential depends first upon your ability to stoke up the burning desire to succeed as a leader. Without that high degree of motivation you'll give up at the first signs of difficulty. That desire is partly a reflection of your level of ability. Mozart passionately wanted to write and play music because he had a genius for it.

If leadership is your vocation you feel you *must* use and develop your gift for it, and you will be unhappy if you do not. But it is also in part a consequence of your commitment to a cause. 'Give me,' said Oliver Cromwell, 'the russet-coated captain who knows what he is fighting for, and loves what he knows.' Your motivation to become a leader can be developed best by finding a sphere of work which you find absorbingly interesting and demandingly worthwhile. Then you will show infectious dedication to the job in hand.

LEARN FROM YOUR MISTAKES

Granted that you are reasonably well motivated to lead and have evolved a programme of self-development (which may involve the help of outside training agencies) in order to prepare yourself for the leadership opportunities awaiting you, there is one contingency that you need to think about in advance – failure. You will certainly encounter it in the exercise of leadership, for there can be no great success unless you are willing sometimes to work on the edge of failure.

Using the Three Circles model and the rest of this book, work hard to diagnose the *cause* of that failure. It may have lain within you, or in circumstances beyond your control. But you need to know. So you must ruthlessly track down the cause of failure as if you were investigating an aeroplane crash. You will not regain your confidence to fly again until you understand what went wrong and know that you have mended the fault in yourself or the organization. As Emerson said, 'A man's success is made up of failures, because he experiments and ventures every day, and the more falls he gets, moves faster on ... I have heard that in horsemanship he is not the good rider who never was thrown, but rather that a man will never be a good rider until he is thrown; then he will not be haunted any longer by the terror that he shall tumble, and will ride whither he is bound.'

Thus, failure can be your best teacher. It can also give you the priceless gift of humility. As the vice-president of an American company once said to me, 'I have had enough success to keep me from despair, and enough failure to keep me humble.'

What you need in order to learn is accurate feedback on the way you are coming across in your role as a leader. The impressions you are giving may not match up with your inner intentions. Look for a pattern in the feedback from superiors, colleagues or subordinates – solicited or unsolicited – that comes your way. Remember the Hungarian saying:

> *When a man says you are a horse laugh at him.*
> *When two men assert that you are a horse, give it a*
> *thought.*
> *And when three men say you are a horse, you had better*
> *go and buy a saddle for yourself.*

If you know the general impression you are giving – be it in the domain of qualities, knowledge or functions – you have the freedom to change your behaviour. Painful as it may be at the time, although it is usually from stinging critical feedback that we learn the most, we come to know that it is only through the eyes of others that we can see our faults. And in time we can appreciate that this painful self-knowledge is a kind of blessing. As the Arabs say: 'When God wishes a man well, he gives him insight into his faults.'

IMAGINE SUCCESS

When it comes to developing your burning desire, remember that *imagination is the leader of willpower*. Schoolchildren day-dream of becoming famous: they visualize themselves as carrying out some heroic exploit or making a great discovery. Purposeful day-dreaming is how nature prepares us for the future. If you want to increase your motivation, start by using your imagination. Picture where you want to be and how you want to behave. Don't give up because you feel you lack sufficient motivation at the moment. Within limits you can do something about that, especially as you come to know better what triggers your own energy most effectively.

The essence of leadership

I mentioned in Chapter 1 that John Buchan gave a great lecture on 'Montrose and Leadership' before the University of St Andrews in 1930. No one has ever put better what he had to say:

'One last word. We may analyse leadership meticulously, like a chemical compound, but we shall never extract its inner essence. There will always be something which escapes us, for in leadership there is a tincture of the miraculous.

I should define the miraculous element as a response of spirit to spirit. There is in all men, even the basest, some kinship with the divine, something which is capable of rising superior to common passions and the lure of easy rewards, superior to pain and loss, superior even to death. The true leader evokes this. The *greatness* in him wins a response, *an answering greatness* in his followers.

Montrose appealed to that god-like something in his rough levies so that even in their cups they followed him blindly. He appealed to that divine something in the Edinburgh mob when, for one moment, bound and despised as he was, he became their leader, and they his followers. You will find it all through history, whether it be the response to the appeal of saints and crusaders and great captains, or Mazzini winning ignorant men to an unselfish ideal, or John Wesley evoking the spiritual power of the rudest and most degraded classes in England.

The task of leadership is not to put greatness into humanity, but to elicit it, for the greatness is already there. I offer you that reflection as my last word on the subject this afternoon. I believe that it is profoundly true. It is a truth which is the basis of all religion. It is a truth which is the only justification for democracy. It is a truth which is the foundation and the hope of our mortal lives.'

Exercise 9: Your leadership vision
Are you confident that you have chosen the right field of
work in which to exercise leadership?

How would you rate your motivation or desire to
improve your own leadership ability?:
    burning fiercely ....
    warm flame ....
    glowing embers ....
    fire seems out ....

Can you already imagine yourself in a senior leadership
position?

Somebody once called golf 'the humbling game'. How much
more so is the exercise of leadership! Here you are competing
essentially against yourself. If you feed upon your strengths
and starve your weaknesses, if you apply the principles of
leadership, your performance as a leader will certainly get
better – but there is always more to be learned.

Once you get to one level, you will espy the next ridge of
quality ahead. You may feel, for example, that you have
mastered the functions of planning, controlling and appraising. But is that the whole of leadership? Another crest looms
up ahead: the ability to inspire. And so it will go on. For
leadership attracts us because it is such an inexhaustible
subject. As you go deeper into it you will see that skill and
technique are not enough by themselves. As Joseph Conrad
said: 'Efficiency of a practical flawless kind may be achieved
naturally in the struggle for bread. But there is something
beyond – a higher point, a subtle and unmistakable touch of
love and pride beyond mere skill; almost an inspiration
which gives to all work that finish which is almost art –
which is art.'

If this book has succeeded, it should have given you at

least some glimpses of what that 'subtle and unmistakable touch of love' means within the context of leadership.

The prayer of a famous leader

Lord, make me an instrument of your peace!
   Where there is hatred, let me sow love,
   Where there is injury, pardon;
   Where there is doubt, faith;
   Where there is despair, hope;
   Where there is darkness, light;
   Where there is sadness, joy.
O Divine Master, grant that I may not so much seek
   to be consoled, as to console;
   to be understood, as to understand;
   to be loved, as to love.
For it is in giving that we receive;
It is in pardoning that we are pardoned;
It is in dying that we are born to eternal life.

Francis of Assisi

I am aware in revising this book that I have tended to stress the challenges, demands and difficulties – even the burdens – of leadership rather a lot. Let me now redress that balance with at least a few gleams of light – the rewards or joys of being a leader. Ann Mansell, an impressive chief executive of a large manufacturing business, once shared her thoughts on leadership with me. What she says is within my reach and yours. You will notice how well it ties in with the Three Circles model and the generic role of leadership. Here is her philosophy.

My obligation as a manager is to manage in a way that enables the needs of the business to be met and the joint objectives of my colleagues and myself to be achieved. In bringing this about I have the responsibility to see that the people responsible to me who are fulfilling the task have the opportunity to extract satisfaction and fun in doing it.

Yes, I do mean fun. Difficult tasks do not preclude enjoyment and fun: when the fun goes out of a job one should seriously consider whether one is equipped to cope – being a manager today certainly requires a sense of humour.

The occasions on which I have gained most personal satisfaction from heading up a team have been when the going has been really tough and yet one is conscious of the enormous support and enthusiasm from that team of people.

I believe, however, that the effort which has to be made by every member of the team in order to achieve that unity of purpose is far greater than any demands which the task in itself could present. It is also far more rewarding. If we try to evaluate that effort against the demands of the task it is like trying to judge whether we would have recovered from pneumonia if we had not taken the unpleasant drugs. We will never know but we are thankful to be still alive. Creating a working environment which gives satisfaction to those operating in it is an objective in itself. This does not imply it should be an easy environment, but it should be a rewarding one in terms of job satisfaction.

Leadership is a mixture of enthusiasm, striving to achieve a goal, maximising resources and enthusing others which adds to the appeal of the successful manager.

A definition which I probably share with many other managers is what true leadership is not about – it is not about power; it is about a person's legitimate right to lead through example and self-discipline. Most of us, at least, recognize it, admire it, and respond when we see it displayed.

Exercise 10: Operation self-development

Choose three objectives from the following list to incorporate in your **leadership self-development programme** over the next five years.

1. To participate in at least two short courses in the field of 'the human side of enterprise', such as public speaking, communication, leadership, interviewing skills or decision making, and creative thinking.
2. To interview formally or informally five proven leaders you respect in order to listen to their ideas on leadership and to learn how they came by them. Not more than three of these leaders should be in your own industry or profession.
3. To ask ten people not in your working group or organization what they value most in their leader's behaviour – and what they value least. Record the answers in your notebook.
4. To read one thought-provoking or stimulating book about leadership or the management of people in each of the five years, recording a minimum of five action points from each.
5. To answer within the next three months the following questions.

   • What are my personal objectives in my working life?
   • What purpose in my life do they serve?
   • What value do I place on attaining those personal objectives?

- When are they going to be accomplished? What is my programme?
- Where do I stand now? Where am I going from here?
- How can I improve my present performance?
- Who are my most helpful advisers and critics?

6. To get accurate assessments of what the organization you work for thinks about your leadership potential. To find out and appraise the organization's programme for developing your potential in this period.
7. To evolve a contingency plan in case your organization does not give you a real opportunity to exercise more leadership in the next five years.
8. If your present job does not give you much chance to develop leadership, or if it does not use all your abilities, choose another field (youth services, community, local government, church, politics, etc.) in which you can add to your track record of leadership. The change of situation should stretch you and stimulate you.
9. Offer to carry out in your own spare time and without charge a leadership survey of a local organization, such as a charity or service, which is not doing very well. Use the Three Circles model to diagnose what is wrong. Come up with an action programme – including a leadership training course – and implement it.
10. Authority flows from the man who knows. Select one course which is going to enhance or widen your professional or technical knowledge on the one hand or your knowledge of management in general – finance, marketing, production, distribution – on the other. Work out a plan for persuading your company that it is in its interests to send you on it.

Which three objectives have you chosen?

Objective no.   Completion date

....

....

....

SUMMARY

Your **leadership self-development programme** should reflect your commitment and burning desire to make the most of your talents. It should focus as much as possible on *practical steps*, for if you do the right things you will become a leader. There is no magic about it, nor is there any recipe for instant success. Do not wait for the right attitudes to appear – that can take years. Actions form attitudes. If you form a picture of the person you would like to be – drawing upon models or examples of real leaders – then all things will begin to work together to grow into that stature.

Experience and theory, success and failure, friend and foe, will all help you in one way or another. Do not be afraid of taking bold initiatives, even risks, with your career, especially if you are aiming high.

The good news is that there is always more about leadership to be learned. No one person knows it all or does it all. What matters most is that you are now moving steadily higher on the path of leadership, setting past failures or disappointments firmly behind you. For the true leader, like Wordsworth's 'Happy Warrior', 'Looks forward, persevering to the last, From well to better, daily self-surpast.'

Within the tapestry of this book I have woven in some threads of colour from my own personal odyssey. Now, as our paths part, let me leave you with some words borrowed from a seventeenth-century German poet.

> *Friends you have read enough.*
> *If you desire still more,*
> *then be the odyssey yourself*
> *and all that it stands for.*

CHECKLIST:
YOUR LEADERSHIP SELF-DEVELOPMENT PROGRAMME

	Yes	No
Have you now drafted a programme of action or growth points which covers the:	☐	☐
short term (tomorrow to one year)?	☐	☐
middle term (one to three years)?	☐	☐
long term (four to ten years)?	☐	☐
Have you entered into your diary some dates for progress reviews?	☐	☐

Can you discuss your plans with anyone at work or outside it to establish if they are

	Yes	No
too ambitious	☐	☐
too modest	☐	☐
too vague	☐	☐
too unrealistic	☐	☐

What would you say has been the key sentence in this book as far as you are concerned? Write it here.

	Yes	No
Are you prepared to read that sentence again in six months time to see if it has had any effect on your leadership?	☐	☐
Have you identified three objectives from the list of ten in the 'Operation self-development' exercise and incorporated them into your programme?	☐	☐

Now turn back to that exercise (page 212) and choose three more for consideration in one year's time – if not already covered in your programme.

ANSWERS TO EXERCISES

EXERCISE 2: Have you got what it takes for a top job in leadership? (page 14)

Ranking of attributes rated most valuable at the top level of management by a cross section of successful chief executives.

1. Ability to take decisions	13. Enterprise
2. Leadership	14. Capacity to speak lucidly
3. Integrity	15. Astuteness
4. Enthusiasm	16. Ability to administer efficiently
5. Imagination	17. Open-mindedness
6. Willingness to work hard	18. Ability to 'stick to it'
7. Analytical ability	19. Willingness to work long hours
8. Understanding of others	20. Ambition
9. Ability to spot opportunities	21. Single-mindedness
10. Ability to meet unpleasant situations	22. Capacity for lucid writing
11. Ability to adapt quickly to change	23. Curiosity
	24. Skill with numbers
12. Willingness to take risks	25. Capacity for abstract thought

EXERCISE 5: Creative solutions (page 93)

1. Many people unconsciously place a framework around the dots. They are making an assumption without realising it. But the problem can only be solved by going outside that invisible, self-imposed barrier, thus:

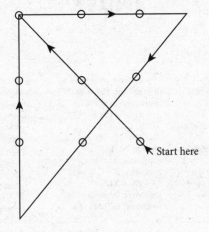

Start here

2. With the six matchsticks, too, people try to solve the problem in two dimensions. The most elegant solution, however, is to break that assumption and build a three-dimensional pyramid. A 'Star of David' arrangement is also acceptable. It involves some creativity, because you are at least putting matchsticks on top of each other, but it is less exciting.

INDEX

222